2-2-10--

ANG LEE

ASIAN AMERICANS
OF ACHIEVEMENT

ASIAN AMERICANS OF ACHIEVEMENT

ANG LEE

CLIFFORD W. MILLS

CHELSEA HOUSE
PUBLISHERS
An imprint of Infobase Publishing

Ang Lee

Copyright © 2009 by Infobase Publishing

Chelsea House
An imprint of Infobase Publishing
132 West 31st Street
New York NY 10001

Library of Congress Cataloging-in-Publication Data
Mills, Cliff, 1947-
  Ang Lee / By Clifford W. Mills.
    p. cm. — (Asian Americans of achievement)
  Includes bibliographical references and index.
  ISBN 978-1-60413-566-4 (hardcover)
  1. Lee, Ang, 1954- 2. Motion picture producers and directors—United States—Biography. I. Title. II. Series.
  PN1998.3.L438M55 2009
  791.4302'33092—dc22
  [B]   2009009916

Chelsea House books are available at special discounts when purchased in bulk quantities for businesses, associations, institutions, or sales promotions. Please call our Special Sales Department in New York at (212) 967-8800 or (800) 322-8755.

You can find Chelsea House on the World Wide Web at http://www.chelseahouse.com

Series design by Erika K. Arroyo
Cover design by Ben Peterson

Printed in the United States of America

Bang EJB 10 9 8 7 6 5 4 3 2 1

This book is printed on acid-free paper.

All links and Web addresses were checked and verified to be correct at the time of publication. Because of the dynamic nature of the Web, some addresses and links may have changed since publication and may no longer be valid.

CONTENTS

Riding on the Magic Red Carpet

"The whole world is watching." One of the few times when this statement is true is Oscar night, when the Academy of Motion Picture Arts and Sciences presents its outstanding film achievement awards. The telecast of the Academy Awards, as the ceremony is also known, draws an astounding number of viewers from almost every country. Even when the glamour and glitz are silly or overdone, many people call it the greatest show on Earth. Oscar night is one of the most watched events every year, drawing almost as many global fans as the World Cup or the Super Bowl.

The 78th Annual Academy Awards took place on March 5, 2006, at the Kodak Theatre in Hollywood, California. The long, black, shiny limousines carrying mega-celebrities, stars, and others invited to the Academy Awards began to arrive at an enormous security tent at the corner of Hollywood Boulevard and Highland Avenue up to three hours before the ceremony started at 5 P.M. local time. "Limo lock" keeps traffic moving slowly, but getting to the theater late is unthinkable. Too much is at stake.

Like many important events after September 11, 2001, the awards ceremony featured security guards everywhere. Some made sure that all of the limousine windows were down so that the people inside could be seen well before they entered the area set aside for metal detectors and wanding (even the rich and famous are checked for weapons). Police helicopters droned overhead. Protesters lined the street because a controversial film had been nominated as "Best Picture," a film named *Brokeback Mountain*. The movie made some people uncomfortable because it dealt with issues surrounding homosexuality and society's conflicted reaction to gay and bisexual men. The protesters were kept away from the theater itself, but they added a layer of tension to what is always a dramatic evening.

THE MAGIC RED CARPET

One by one and two by two, Hollywood's elite stepped out of their limos onto the famous red carpet. It is no ordinary carpet—it is luxurious and enormous, stretching endlessly away from Hollywood Boulevard toward the Kodak Theatre. It has been called "magic" because for some of the people walking it for the first time, it makes a dream come true; it fulfills a wish made in childhood—to go to Hollywood and become a movie star. The magic carpet seems to change color with the light. It starts as fire-engine red in the afternoon, turns dark cranberry as the daylight fades, and seems almost purple when lit only by strong artificial lights at night.

Keira Knightley, Jessica Alba, Salma Hayek, Will Smith, Will Ferrell, and Steve Carell were just a few of the stars on the red carpet for the 78th Oscars. Closer to the start of the ceremony, George Clooney, Nicole Kidman, Jennifer Aniston, and Meryl Streep arrived. The bigger the star, the later his or her arrival.

Ang Lee and his wife, Jane Lin, walked the red carpet on their way into the Kodak Theatre for the 78th Annual Academy Awards on March 5, 2006, in Hollywood, California. Lee was nominated for "Best Director" for his work on the film *Brokeback Mountain*.

One of the most talked-about couples was a young actor named Heath Ledger and his date, Michelle Williams. Her bright yellow gown highlighted her blond hair and red lipstick, making her much more glamorous than her role in *Brokeback*

Mountain. Similarly, Ledger's black-tie tuxedo contrasted with the cowboy garb he wore in *Brokeback.* They seemed both chic and down-to-earth at the same time, the symbols of a new generation of Hollywood actors.

Soon after Ledger and Williams, another couple arrived—the director Ang Lee and his wife, Jane Lin. They were both dressed in black, and both seemed only slightly awed by the spectacle around them, as flashbulbs went off and the screams of fans pierced through the sounds of traffic, horns, and chants of protesters. They held hands tightly as they stepped onto the carpet. Lee was the director of *Brokeback Mountain* and had just come through the gauntlet of protesters, so he must have been relieved to see more friendly faces. He and his wife had had trouble getting to the awards—their plane had been caught in a late-winter storm in New York and its wings needed to be de-iced several times before it could take off. Many developments would make this night unforgettable for them.

SWEPT ONTO EGO ALLEY

The magic red carpet actually forks after the security tent into two paths headed for the Kodak. The right path is for the movie people who are not celebrities, those who care for and carry the cameras, set up and use the sound equipment, and make lower-level decisions about film sites and schedules. They do much of the work to make this most complicated art form possible. The other path is called "Ego Alley," and is taken not only by celebrities but also by studio executives who would not be caught dead taking the path of the less famous. This longer route to the theater goes by the 375 credentialed reporters, photographers, and TV interviewers. It is where the cameras, fame, and fortune await.

Ang Lee and Jane Lin followed others onto Ego Alley. This 500-foot (152-meter) walk from the security tent to the theater is the thrill of a lifetime for many. Even experienced stars say that they are still excited by the amount of attention and publicity. Lee and Lin did not seem to love the attention, and they did not pause every few feet for an interview or a photo. But they also appeared poised and calm, smiling and waving politely.

What happened next is described by the writer of the short story "Brokeback Mountain." Her name is Annie Proulx, and she wrote about that evening in an article for an English newspaper:

> The red carpet in front of the theater was larger than the Red Sea. Inside, we climbed grand staircases designed for showing off dresses. The circular levels [of the Kodak Theatre] filled with men in black, the women mostly in pale, frothy gowns. . . . More exquisite dresses appeared every moment, some made from six yards of taffeta, and many with sweeping trains.

Entertainment reporters would later note that, as usual, the stars did not dare hug one another—hair and makeup were too complicated for that. Air kisses are all that are allowed. They would also note that life on Ego Alley is expensive: Dolly Parton's earrings were worth $1.2 million, and Jennifer Garner had to have special ear piercings to carry her $250,000 earrings, which resembled small chandeliers filled with diamonds. Publicists listed the items in the gift bags given to the 99 performers in the awards show: iPods, vacation gift certificates, a silk kimono, a pearl necklace, surfing lessons, spa treatments, and much more—worth more than $100,000. 2006 was the last year for such gift bags—the Internal Revenue Service ruled that they were not gifts but income, and taxable. George Clooney donated his to the United Way.

A MIX OF THE COMIC AND SERIOUS

Finally, after sipping champagne in the Kodak lobby and admiring each other's gowns and appearance, everyone was seated—all 3,300 of those lucky enough to be invited. The opening skit was a parody of a scene in *Brokeback Mountain,* featuring Billy Crystal and Chris Rock. Host Jon Stewart was shown awakening in a bed with Halle Barry and then falling back asleep. When he woke again, he was lying alongside George Clooney, who told him he was not dreaming and the show must start. And so it did.

Clooney won one of the early awards, for "Best Actor in a Supporting Role," and gave an acceptance speech that turned serious. He had heard all the jokes about *Brokeback Mountain's* gay cowboys and had seen the protesters outside railing against the evils of homosexuality and the "Hollywood agenda." Critics were proclaiming that Hollywood was out of touch with the rest of America. Clooney's speech was a powerful defense:

> And finally, I would say that, you know, we are a little bit out of touch in Hollywood every once in a while. I think it's probably a good thing. We're the ones who talked about AIDS when it was just being whispered, and we talked about civil rights when it wasn't really popular. . . . This academy, this group of people, gave Hattie McDaniel [a black actress in the famous movie *Gone With the Wind*] an Oscar in 1939 when blacks were still sitting in the backs of theaters. I'm proud to be a part of this academy.

Other winners came to the stage to accept their Oscars: Philip Seymour Hoffman for his role in *Capote* and Reese Witherspoon for her role in *Walk the Line.* Both were playing real people, Truman Capote and June Carter Cash, one of the few times in Oscar history when the two top acting awards went for performances depicting actual people. Larry McMurtry and Diana Ossana had taken Annie Proulx's short story and adapted it into the script for *Brokeback Mountain,* and they won the Oscar for "Best Writing—Adapted Screenplay." The tension was mounting for the last two awards, the two biggest of the night, "Best Director" and "Best Picture."

THE FIRST ASIAN-AMERICAN "BEST DIRECTOR"

When Ang Lee heard his name read as the winner of the "Best Director" award, he stood up and hugged his wife, smiled broadly, and shook hands with one of the other stars of the movie, Jake Gyllenhaal. He mounted the stairs to the stage, walked into a blur of applause, shouts, and instant fame. He accepted his Oscar, clutching it with both hands, and began a moving speech, part of which was in Mandarin Chinese:

> I want to thank two people who don't even exist. Their names are Ennis and Jack, and they taught all of us who made *Brokeback Mountain* so much about not just the gay men and women whose love is denied by society, but just as important, the greatness of love itself. . . . Thank you members of the academy for this great honor. . . . And finally to my mother and family and everybody in Taiwan, Hong Kong, and China . . . *Xiexie dajia de guanxin* [Thank you for caring].

His wife beamed up at him. He looked at her and said, "I love you. On *Brokeback,* I felt you with me every day." He also looked out at the audience and quietly said, "I just did this movie after my father passed away. More than any other, I made this for him." Several audience members began to cry.

The 78th Academy Awards were being broadcast live in Lee's home country of Taiwan, at 9 A.M. on March 6, 2006.

Ang Lee gives his acceptance speech at the Academy Awards in 2006. He was the first Asian American to win an Oscar as "Best Director."

Millions of television sets were tuned in to see if Lee would become the first Asian American to win the "Best Director" award. Cries of joy could be heard throughout Taipei City when Lee's name was read, and that joy did not diminish for days. Chinese newspapers called him "The Glory of Asia." The government-controlled English-language newspaper in China described him as "the pride of Chinese people all over the world." Ironically, *Brokeback Mountain* had not been approved

WHO IS OSCAR?

Oscar is famous. His official name is "Academy Award of Merit," and he can be found in the homes of many of the most prestigious people in the film industry (sometimes as a doorstop, sometimes as the centerpiece of the house). But who and what is Oscar, and how did he get his name?

Oscar is an 8½-pound and 13½-inch-tall (3.85-kilogram and 34.2-centimeter-tall) trophy, made of gold-plated solid metal (now britannium, similar to pewter), sitting on a black metal base. He is a knight holding a crusader's sword and standing on a reel of film with five spokes. Each spoke represents a branch of the Academy of Motion Picture Arts and Sciences: actors, writers, directors, producers, and technicians.

In the early days of the Academy Awards, from 1929 to 1933, Oscar had no name. Then, in 1934, many people began to refer to the statuette as "Oscar," but no one is quite sure why. Legend has it that an academy librarian named Margaret Herrick saw the statue and said, "That looks just like my uncle Oscar!" Actress Bette Davis also claimed credit for naming Oscar after her first husband. In 1939, the academy made the name official.

Each Oscar is made by hand at the R.S. Owens Company in Chicago. If one shows an imperfection, it is sawed in half and melted down. For years, Oscars had been shipped to Hollywood by truck, but when a load of the statuettes (55 in six boxes weighing 470 pounds, or 213 kilograms) was stolen from a Los Angeles loading dock in 2000, the academy made changes. Oscars are now flown on a special flight from Chicago to Los Angeles and kept under guard.

Walt Disney is the record holder for most Oscars won: 26. He also holds the record for number of Oscar nominations: 64.

for showing in China. But young Internet surfers had begun to download bootleg copies of the movie and shared them online.

A MOMENT LATER, DISAPPOINTMENT

Jack Nicholson was the last presenter of the night, for the "Best Picture" award. When he read the name of the winner, *Crash*, a gasp went up around the theater and backstage. Most people had assumed that *Brokeback* would win. Journalists later speculated that some of the 6,000 academy members had simply been too afraid to vote for such a controversial movie. When asked at a news conference why his movie did not win, Lee only said, "You're asking me a question, and I don't know the answer. . . . Congratulations to the *Crash* filmmakers." He impressed many with his calm expression and willingness to accept the loss so gracefully. He was clearly disappointed but did not let that show for more than an instant.

Soon after, Lee and Jane Lin, with Heath Ledger and Michelle Williams, headed to an after-awards party given by *Vanity Fair* magazine. They joined Jake Gyllenhaal and hundreds of others. This time getting past security would be no problem—Lee was now more famous than he had ever been. They celebrated most of the night, until the party ended at 3 A.M., and they must have drowned any sorrows about *Brokeback Mountain* not winning the "Best Picture" award. When all the lights were turned off in front of the Kodak, the magic red carpet lost all of its color and was put away for next year.

EXPLORING MANY CULTURES AND GENERATIONS

Ang Lee's "Best Director" award was recognition of not just his work on one movie, but on all of his films. He is an extraordinary director because he treats the clashes of cultures and generations with insight and he beautifully uses sight and sound to capture people, places, and ideas.

Lee has taken chances with his art, refusing to stick to one genre of movie like his idol Alfred Hitchcock (who specialized in thrillers). He takes chances with his actors, directing several now-famous stars when they were still very young and relatively inexperienced: Tobey Maguire, Christina Ricci, Katie Holmes, Kate Winslet, and Zhang Ziyi all gave remarkable performances early in their careers under Lee's direction. Heath Ledger, Jake Gyllenhaal, and Michelle Williams were all nominated for Academy Awards for their work on *Brokeback,* one of the youngest casts in Hollywood history to receive three nominations. Lee has also directed many experienced actors and prodded them into giving some of the finest performances of their careers: Kevin Kline, Emma Thompson, Hugh Grant, Joan Allen, Michelle Yeoh, Chow Yun-Fat, and Sigourney Weaver all played roles in Lee films that brought them further international recognition.

His films mirror many societies, from nineteenth-century England to China in the 1930s to America in the 1960s and 1970s. He captures the sights and sounds of Chinatown in New York City, the suburban landscape of New Canaan (Connecticut), the Rocky Mountains, and the English countryside in the early 1800s. Because of his insistence on accurate details of any time and place, audiences are more easily drawn into his movies. They suspend their disbelief.

Lee's films have become part of many cultures. He has made films in English, Taiwanese, and Mandarin Chinese. His movie *Crouching Tiger, Hidden Dragon* is still the most successful foreign-language film ever released in the United States. It won four Oscars.

A 14-YEAR OVERNIGHT SUCCESS

Lee's mastery of film technique did not come easily or overnight. He is a study in how someone can bloom later in life. His genius took time to develop. Lee arrived in the United States from Taiwan at the age of 23, but he did not make his

Ang Lee's brother, Khan Lee, pumped his fist after Ang won the "Best Director" award at the 2006 Oscars ceremony. Their mother, 81-year-old Shu Zwan Yang, was seated next to Khan Lee. People throughout Taiwan rejoiced over Ang Lee's victory.

first movie until he was 37. He had not been a model son or student in Taiwan and had failed his university exams twice. He had embarrassed his father by becoming an actor and not an engineer. In America, he struggled to get a job as a script-writer, actor, or assistant director, and was rejected by almost every studio in Hollywood and New York. His wife supported him throughout his "lost years," even stopping him from taking a low-level job in computers that would have put an end to his dream of working in film. Like many late bloomers, he was supported by someone who believed in him. Jane Lin did not believe in him as a director or an actor or a writer, she just believed in him as a person.

Lee has become a creative genius who is so deeply involved in his movies that each one changes him. He is attracted to subjects that many people want to avoid: race, gender, sexual orientation, class, and difficult and harmful relationships. He wants to learn through his movies and carry that knowledge to audiences. He always wants to know more, to explore more. And he does not like to repeat himself—most film critics point out that each of Lee's movies is quite different from the one before and after. He explained his moviemaking philosophy in an interview with journalist Oren Moverman:

> Every time I make a new film now, I think it's going to be a flop, that my number is up, and I like that. I don't want to fail, but I do want to see where the edge is—that's my attitude toward film. But I don't want to be a slave to moviemaking. I'll do what I have to do to make it work, but once a film is done, it's time to move one notch higher. To me, directing is about learning, life is about learning. Learning is not a way of getting your goal—it's the goal itself.

His story is a remarkable one. Lee is not the typical Hollywood director wielding power from a lavish home with big parties and luxurious cars. He lives in a modest house in Larchmont, New York, not Hollywood, and he drives the same minivan he has had for years. Like many creative geniuses, Lee does not see the need to become materialistic: his ideas excite him, not his things. His remarkable life has roots in China, and begins in Taiwan, half a world away from Hollywood and New York.

Growing Up Taiwanese

Ang Lee's story begins with his grandparents, who were landowners in the Jiangxi Province in southeastern China. This beautiful area is bounded by mountains on three sides, and is south of the Yangtze River. It is noted for its wild places (the show *Survivor* was once shot there) and its strongly flavored cuisine. The region also has a very long history, like all of China, stretching back millennia, not just centuries. Its past is still with us.

A revolutionary leader named Mao Zedong started a Communist Party government in the area in the early 1930s, challenging China's national government, led by General Chiang Kai-shek and his Kuomintang party (the KMT). Mao Zedong's Communists became popular, especially with poor people in rural areas who were most vulnerable to starvation and attacks from Japanese forces occupying China. After the end of World War II, an open civil war broke out in China, pitting the nationalist Kuomintang party forces against the Communist forces.

People on sampans (flat-bottomed boats) squeezed closer to the mouth of the Yangtze River in Shanghai, China, in December 1948, as refugees fled from Communist troops advancing on the city. China was in the midst of a civil war between the Communists and the nationalists.

The KMT was partly brought down by its economic policies, which included printing too much worthless money. A sack of rice cost 12 yuan in 1937 and 63 million yuan by the end of 1948. People wanting to buy groceries had to bring their cash in wheelbarrows. KMT money was literally worth less than the paper it was printed on.

Lee's grandparents (his father's parents) were victims in this civil war. At some point, Communist forces killed them because, as landowners, they were seen as part of the nationalist establishment. Many peasants had felt exploited by landowners, and they wanted their revenge. In many cases, they got it.

STARTING OVER

In May 1949, the Communists seized control of China's biggest city, Shanghai. People not in the Communist Party began to flee, often sewing gold and jewelry into their clothes and leaving businesses and homes. Many had to cling to the tops and sides of crowded railroad cars, throwing away suitcases filled with family treasures that would not fit on the trains. Some went to the United States, and some went to Hong Kong,

CHINA AND TAIWAN

When Mao Zedong and the Communist forces won control of Mainland China in 1949, the whole world was shocked. Rarely in history has the globe's most populous country changed governments from one form to a completely different form. The leader of the Kuomintang, Chiang Kai-shek, and 2 million Chinese nationalists left Mainland China for the island of Taiwan. The Chinese-American community was split, with some offering support for Communist China (formally called the People's Republic of China or PRC), and others favoring the Taiwan government led by Chiang Kai-shek (formally called the Nationalist Republic of China or just the Republic of China, or ROC).

The U.S. government was at first unwavering in its support for Taiwan and its campaign against PRC sympathizers in the United States. Many Chinese Americans suspected of supporting the PRC found their mail opened and their phones tapped, and some waited for the knock on the door meaning a long interrogation by FBI or other officials.

Several events, however, changed the balance of power between China and Taiwan. Communist China developed an atomic a territory on the Chinese mainland that was then under British rule. Many went to an island off the southeast coast of China, an island named "Formosa" ("beautiful") by Portuguese explorers centuries before and now called Taiwan. In December 1949, Chiang Kai-shek retreated to Taiwan, with what was left of his nationalist army, along with many government workers and a great deal of gold bullion. He formed a new Chinese government in Taiwan, creating a "second China" that exists to this day.

Two of the people to leave the mainland for Taiwan in 1949 were Lee Sheng and Shu Zwan Yang, Ang Lee's father and

bomb in the 1960s, making it more of a force on the global stage. U.S. President Richard Nixon famously visited the People's Republic of China in February 1972, giving it more world recognition and leading the United Nations to grant the PRC a seat, replacing Taiwan. Finally, in 1979, President Jimmy Carter formally recognized what the rest of the world had by then taken for granted as Communist China grew into an economic powerhouse: The PRC was the official government of China, and the Taiwan government was not. The worst fear of the Taiwanese had come true: They were no longer a recognized world power. Taiwanese publisher Antonio Chiang told *New York Times* reporter Nicholas Kristof, "We [the Taiwanese] don't know who we are. . . . We don't know what we'll be in the future, an independent country, a part of China or whatever. It's an unreal existence."

China's successful hosting of the 2008 Olympics showed how far it had come as a world power. Its "century of shame and humiliation" (as some Chinese textbooks call the 100 years before 1949) is over. Taiwan is still split from China, but many think the differences between the Mainland Chinese and the Taiwanese are fading as China becomes more like Taiwan.

mother. Lee Sheng was the only member of his entire family to escape alive.

Lee Sheng met Shu Zwan Yang while she was teaching at an elementary school, and they soon married. Lee Sheng became a teacher and a school administrator, and the newlyweds started a family after moving to Pingtung County, an agricultural area in the southern part of Taiwan.

Their first children were twin girls, named Wen and Ren. Then, on October 23, 1954, their first son was born, in the town of Chaochou. They named him Ang. Soon after, another son, Khan, was born. The Lee family was growing. The family was large and prestigious enough to have a cook, a gardener, and a housekeeper.

ESCAPING INTO IMAGINATION

Like many creative children in a strict household and in a some-what repressive culture, Ang Lee found ways to escape. Sheltered by his bedroom's blue walls, he began to imagine whole scenes. He often daydreamed about faraway places and martial-arts fights. Yet he was rarely in those scenes—others were having the adventures, not him. Gazing out of his bedroom window toward a chicken coop made of bamboo, he could transform it in his mind's eye.

Ang had to control and repress his feelings. He could not let them show, or there would be consequences. The repressed feelings made him seem shy and unexpressive. He seemed detached and forgetful. He would often leave his schoolbag on the bus. At lunch, he "was so spaced out I fell back in my chair, literally tipped over." He was clumsy, unathletic, and socially awkward. He was an outsider.

There was another place where Lee felt he could escape with his imagination—the movie theater. When watching movies, he suddenly became overwhelmed with emotions. He especially loved martial-arts movies, where emotions were translated into actions. When leaving a movie theater, he often felt that he was a different person from the one who went into it.

A MOVIE THAT CHANGED A LIFE

When he was nine, living with his family in the village of Hwalian on Taiwan's east coast, Lee went to a movie that changed his life: *Liang Shan Bo Yu Zhu Ying Tai*, loosely translated as *Love Eternal*. The film is based on a famous Chinese opera and tells the story of two lovers. It takes place in a fantasy version of

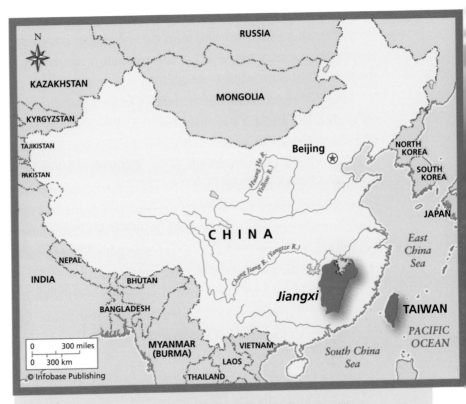

After the Communists took over China in 1949, about 2 million nationalists followed their leader Chiang Kai-shek to Taiwan. Before fleeing to Taiwan, Ang Lee's mother and father lived the province of Jiangxi in China. Ang Lee's father was the only member of his family to survive the civil war.

China, a place of sparkling streams, rich houses, and forest pagodas (a pagoda is a tall tower with a distinctive steeple, usually a shrine, found throughout Asia).

The movie's plot is complicated. Le Di is a young woman living a miserable and sheltered life in a small town. She persuades her strict parents to let her attend a school in a nearby city, but she must go disguised as a boy because girls are not allowed to study. She meets a boy, Ling Po, at a streamside pagoda, and they quickly become friends, sharing all the adventures that living at a new school brings. Le Di falls in love with Ling Po but cannot find a way to tell him that she is a girl. When she returns home for school vacation, she finds that her father has promised her in marriage to the son of a local wealthy family. She is devastated but cannot disobey her father.

Ling Po learns that his best friend is really a girl and travels to find her and ask her to marry him. When he finds out that she is already promised to another, he becomes sick with a bloody cough that wracks his body. Suddenly, he dies. On the day she is to be married, Le Di takes the bridal party by her true love's grave and tears off her wedding gown to reveal funeral clothes underneath. A sudden storm drives the others away, while opening her lover's grave. She joins his spirit and, reunited, they fly to the gates of a heavenly paradise.

Lee would later tell *New York Times* interviewer Rick Lyman, "*Love Eternal* is not the greatest movie ever made. But there is something so honest and straightforward about it. I cry. I always cry. But I watch it for that feeling, the feeling of the innocence of watching a movie and wanting to believe." Lee recalls crying so loudly that the other people in his row suddenly stopped their own crying to see who was making so much noise. The emotions he could not express at his house came pouring out in the darkness of the theater.

Lee also remembers being struck by something the movie seemed to be saying. Usually, in Chinese movies of the time, the parents were very wise and almost always right. In this movie, they were not. The only person who sees clearly is the young heroine, Le Di. Her parents are partly responsible for destroying her life.

The movie became a significant event in the cultural life of Taiwan at the time. Some packed up box lunches and went to the theater all day. Even Ang Lee's parents were caught up in it, leaving the children on the night a typhoon hit to see the movie for the third time. People who had left Mainland China missed their homeland, and the movie brought back some of its lost culture.

For Lee, the movie also represented a whole new class of film; these were movies devoted to feelings, to love. The class or genre known as kung-fu or martial-arts movies now had a rival for his attentions and affections. And slowly but surely, his childhood sense of wonder would become his profession.

EDUCATING AN IMAGINATION

Like most people, Ang Lee is partly a product of his early education. Since the government of Taiwan claimed to be the real government of all of China, students in Taiwan studied all things Chinese, not Taiwanese. As a student, he spoke Mandarin Chinese, not the Taiwan dialect that existed before the "mainlanders" came to Taiwan in 1949.

As a child and young adult, Lee studied in great depth two threads of Chinese philosophy: Confucianism and Taoism. They are both ancient and complicated systems of moral and religious ideas that are somehow still relevant to modern lives. Confucianism tends to deal with outwardly proper behavior, and Taoism tries to explain ways to achieve inner peace. They seem to agree that the more possessions one has, the more one has to worry about. Both stress the importance of friendship, and both have a guiding principle that you should not do something to another person that you don't want that person to do

(continues on page 30)

Story of My Family

JUST LIKE AN IRISH FAMILY

Ang Lee told writer John Lahr that his father, Lee Sheng, was devastated when he arrived in Taiwan. "He felt very lonely. He had to start the Lee family again. In his generation, there was lots of insecurity, because they'd seen everything disappear and people get killed." Lee later told another interviewer that "my parents had no sense of security. It was as if the world could turn against them at any moment."

Lee sat down with *Interview* magazine journalist Oren Moverman in 1997 and was asked about the story of his family. Lee said:

> Family life to me is very solid. It provides beliefs that can keep you from boredom, from being destructive. . . . Because Chinese society is a patriarchal society, I have always thought the father figure has bigger meaning than just the parent—it's the symbol of how tradition works. . . . My father's entire family was executed in China, but he escaped—he was the only one. He came to Taiwan, where he married my mother and they had me. He was the principal at my high school. . . . It was always embarrassing to be the principal's son! And I was the first son, so I always felt everything rested on my shoulders. There was no love of art or creativity, not to mention the entertainment business, in our family. The whole father thing, family duty—it made it hard to breathe, hard to face your true self.

David Schwartz, curator of the Museum of the Moving Image, interviewed Lee in June 2003 and asked him about his early movies, dealing with Asian-American families and the subtle conflicts between generations. Lee responded, "People come and say, 'Oh, it's just like an Irish family.' 'It's just like an Italian family.' We don't verbalize it, the Chinese. But there is something unique and universal about the process we're going through." Lee says he is always interested in family dramas that explore the conflict between personal desires and family obligations. The bonds between family members can sometimes seem like bondage.

Lee Sheng was a strict father, expecting his children to obey him just as his students would. Ang Lee described his father to Lahr:

> He'd finish [dinner] in five minutes and leave the table. You'd be praying he wouldn't talk. If he talks, it's about something you'd have to be worried about.... I'd really get on his nerves. What would happen? A yell, a smack, whatever. I'd get scared. I'd behave. Then, after a while, I'd drift away again. . . . The way I grew up, you take orders until one day you're old enough to give orders.

In a house with a strict father, there is often little debate or explanation. Lee's father was a man of few words, and he demanded unquestioning respect. But, like many children with a controlling father, Lee had a mother with whom he could connect. He later described her as "good-tempered, reliant, subordinate, and nervous" and has always seen himself as much more like his mother. He could share his thoughts with her, as well as his feelings.

Lee is now the father of two boys, and he says he sees himself as a different kind of parent from what his father was. When asked more about his own role as a father, he told Moverman, "Children push you to be more mature, but you're never prepared to be a role model and teach kids what to do and give them what they want. . . . You always fear you're not good enough. . . . But as a parent, you have to keep things in order."

Lee went on to say more about parenting:

> The Chinese believe that, if you do something wrong and nothing happens to you, it just means it's not time yet. Being parents, of course, we are sensitive to the question of what we are doing to our children. . . . We think of the consequences. We've got to be careful about what we do for our own convenience . . . because all of that affects our children. . . . Movies and my family are the most important things to me. I try to keep them balanced, but my family has made sacrifices for my work.

(continued from page 27)

to you (a variation on the golden rule of "Do unto others as you would have them do unto you").

Confucian values tend to emphasize the importance of the group over the individual. In fact, there is no Chinese word or character for "individual." People need to limit their own interests for the sake of the larger community. Confucians stress a commitment to education—scholars are the highest rung of the social ladder for them, not the rich and famous. They also stress loyalty to one's family members. People of great wealth are not always to be admired—merchants are the lowest rung of the Confucian social ladder and sometimes are even portrayed as parasites. Ideally, each person knows his or her place in a social order and each person shows complete respect to parents (especially fathers).

Taoist values explore the "tao," translated as "the way." Taoist believers emphasize individual freedom and spontaneity more than Confucian believers do. They value calmness and tranquility. The Taoist says, "I desire not to desire." They also do not believe in boasting: "Those who know don't talk about it; those who talk about it don't know."

Lee would later have to deal with many people not trained in either way of Chinese thinking, people showered with fame, money, and material goods who want a great amount of attention paid to them. His education could not prepare him for understanding all kinds of people, and their needs and feelings. For that, he would need life experience. Two moves to big cities would give him just that.

MOVING TO TAINAN AND HIGH SCHOOL

The Lee family moved from the sleepy village of Hwalian to the much larger city of Tainan, located on the southwestern coast of Taiwan, in a rice-growing region. Tainan is the fourth-largest city on the island, home to roughly 800,000 people. It is also one of Taiwan's oldest cities (at least 400 years old), famous for its Chinese temples with curved red-tile roofs.

Lee's father became the principal of the area's most prestigious school, the Tainan First Senior High School. Only the top students in the area can pass its admissions tests. The school is a small cluster of low-rise brick buildings, and students are expected to wear uniforms—khaki pants and short-sleeved shirts with the school name.

Reporter Min Lee went to Tainan to research what Ang Lee's life was like during this period:

> Lee studied in classrooms packed with tiny chairs and desks. The only relief from the sweltering, sticky heat was rotating-blade fans hanging from the ceiling. . . . His class photo shows him with a crew cut that's shorter than his classmates'. Fellow student George Wang recalled that Lee shied away from overly physical activity. He said Lee was an above average but unremarkable student. Lee always found time for reading novels outside the curriculum—and watching movies. . . . In high school, the stakes were higher for Lee. He was studying both for academic success and family honor.

Since Taiwan has a very competitive educational system, Lee would have been expected to study hard for the challenging college-entrance exams. He would then be on the path toward becoming an engineer. Lee's younger brother, Khan, told Min Lee, "The only purpose of life was to get into college. Because our father was the principal, the other people in his social circle were principals, teachers. There was . . . pressure."

Ang, however, wanted to do more than just study: He drew comics, sang in the choir, and frequently went to the Chin Men Theater, a yellow brick building in Tainan that now has a poster of Lee hanging in it. There, he tried to escape the pressure of being successful in a way that his society expected. He knew he did not love math and engineering, but the expectation that he would become an engineer or a scientist surrounded him. He even felt it hard to breathe sometimes.

THE FIRST CRISIS OF A YOUNG LIFE

Finally, the time came for Lee to take his college-entrance exams. His whole life had been pointing to this test. He failed. He

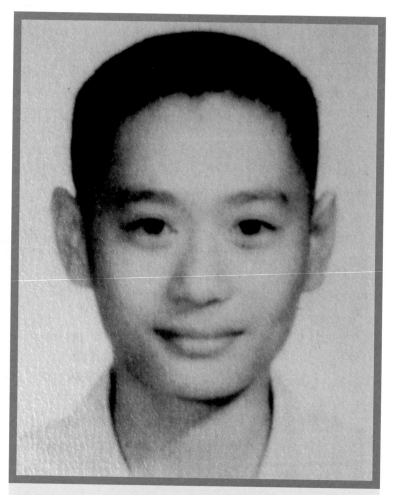

A school photo shows Ang Lee as a 15-year-old. His father, a strict man, was the principal of his high school, and Ang felt much pressure to excel academically. Ang's first big crisis came when he twice failed Taiwan's rigorous college-entrance exams.

told John Lahr, "I was too frightened, I think. I almost blacked out." He took the exams over and failed again. He still has nightmares about the experiences—taking math exams and not knowing the right answers. He still wakes up sweating.

Lee's father, family, and friends were deeply disappointed. Lee felt like a failure, a complete loser with no hopes for the future. His whole life had taken him down a road that ended abruptly. He was in the middle of his first major personal crisis.

The word *crisis* has in its Greek origins the word *decision*, and it was time to make the first big decision of his life. He could either take the exams a third time, enter the military, or go to a vocational school and pursue his passion, theater and film studies. He made the right decision.

At the age of 18, Lee entered the Taiwan Academy of Arts in Taipei, the capital city of Taiwan. He became a theater and film student at the three-year vocational school (now the National Taiwan University of Arts). His father could not imagine a lowlier course of study or profession. Lee told reporter Jennifer Frey, "My culture doesn't regard acting highly. It's shameful to be an entertainer."

TURNING FAILURE INTO SUCCESS

Living in Taipei proved to be an exciting and enlightening experience. Taipei was a true international city, filled with art cinemas, shopping malls, and American/Western influences of many kinds. The city reached a population of more than 2 million in 1975, and it now has the world's tallest building—the Taipei 101 Tower. In Taipei, some students thought of themselves as world citizens, not Chinese or Taiwanese. They could define themselves by their interests—African drum music, computer games, a Japanese band, and Indian food—and not their place of birth.

(continues on page 36)

Other Notable Individuals

TAIWANESE AMERICANS

The world has benefited from many high-achieving Taiwanese Americans. The first Taiwan-born Nobel Prize winner was Yuan Tseh Lee, who won the prize in chemistry in 1986 while teaching at the University of California, Berkeley. In 1994, he returned to Taiwan. He has been called "The Conscience of Taiwan" because of his calls for leaders there to embrace honesty and distance themselves from hatred. In 2000, he declined to be nominated to be premier of the Republic of China so he could devote himself to recruiting more scientists to the research center Academia Sinica in Taipei.

Chang-Lin Tien was the first Asian American to head a major U.S. university. Tien and his parents escaped the Chinese Civil War in 1949. Tien was 14, and his family of 12 lived in one room in Taiwan. The family members had to take turns sleeping. Tien graduated from National Taiwan University and then applied to 240 universities in the United States. One gave him a scholarship, the University of Louisville in Kentucky. He arrived in the United States in 1956, and as soon as he ended his 72-hour bus ride from Seattle to Louisville, he noticed that the bathroom doors were marked "Whites Only" and "Colored." He did not know which to use. Eventually, Tien became a mechanical engineer. He helped design the Saturn booster rocket, heat shields on the space shuttle, and high-speed magnetic-levitation trains. In addition, he served as the chancellor of the University of California, Berkeley, from 1990 to 1997.

One of the most influential scientists in the United States is Samuel Ting, who was born in Michigan to Chinese parents. He was home-schooled in Taiwan before going to high school in Taipei and attending college in Tainan City and at the University of Michigan. He won a Nobel Prize in 1976 for co-discovering a subatomic particle and gave his acceptance speech in Chinese, the first Nobel Prize recipient to do so. Ting, who teaches at the Massachusetts Institute of Technology, has devised one of the most expensive scientific experiments in history, using a 15,000-pound (6,800-kilogram) cosmic ray detector to look for antimatter. The core of the detector is a two-ton super-cooled magnet to be sent into outer space. He and his team are waiting for room for his detector on a NASA space shuttle or some other space vehicle.

David Lee was one of the founders of the computer revolution. Lee's family also left China for Taiwan during the Chinese Civil War in 1949, and the 12-year-old Lee had only the clothes on his back and two silver dollars in his shoes. He worked his way though Montana State University as a janitor and a dishwasher, and earned an engineering degree at North Dakota State University. He designed the first electronic calculator keyboard and then went to California as part of a start-up company called Diablo. In 1972, the Xerox Corporation bought Diablo, making Lee a multimillionaire. He was not able, however, to become a top executive at Xerox, since Asian Americans at the time were often not considered capable of being effective managers. Many found their careers stalled at a certain corporate level, and some began to talk about a "bamboo ceiling." Lee was given a manager who knew little about printers. So, Lee showed his new boss as much as he could, then resigned and cofounded the Qume Corporation. Qume became the largest printer company in the world, as well as the largest manufacturer of disk drives in the United States. Lee helped the computer industry in Taiwan grow by giving work to manufacturers there. The island became a major exporter of personal computers.

Writer Iris Chang notes that most of the highly educated immigrants from Taiwan in the 1960s and 1970s wanted to become college professors or work at large companies like IBM. They wanted secure jobs. A few like Ang Lee were natural risk-takers who knew they could always fall back on their education if their start-up companies failed. Lee didn't fail.

(continued from page 33)

Lee loved becoming an actor at the academy. He told Frey, "Once I acted on stage, I just knew that was my niche." He told National Public Radio's Scott Simon that he remembers the first feelings of being on stage: "I have to first breathe in, take on the audience sitting in the dark, and the spotlight shining on my face and saying the lines, projecting myself. I found the power there." He may have shouted his first lines instead of saying them, but after some training and experience, he started to shine. He told John Lahr that "I was actually good at it. I made sense. When I stood onstage, I felt very tall. I wasn't shy. I got results." He became one of the best actors at the academy, and he even began to win prizes for his performances. He had turned failure into success by finding his true self. He could breathe again.

One advantage of being at the academy was that Lee got to see and study films from Europe and Japan for the first time. He listed the movies that made the biggest impact on him when he was a student: Ingmar Bergman's *Virgin Spring*, Vittorio De Sica's *Bicycle Thief*, Yasujiro Ozu's *Tokyo Story*, and Michelangelo Antonioni's *Eclipse*. An American movie, *The Graduate*, affected him as much as any other. He watched it three times in a row, dazzled by both the subject matter and the technique of the director, Mike Nichols. These movies did not make quite the enormous impression that *Love Eternal* did, but they became part of his working knowledge. He started to notice how movies were constructed, not just the effects they had. He began to be a real student of film, noting how the setting and people are framed in a scene, when the close-ups of actors come, and what an actor is doing when he or she is not speaking.

He soon made two short movies as part of his studies and realized how much he also liked directing. One was an 18-minute silent movie about a kite, somewhat like the famous *American Beauty* sequence showing a plastic bag blowing in the wind, reminding viewers to look for beauty in everyday things. Lee was the director, cameraman, and editor. He found he was able to do on film what he had been doing in his head since childhood: create moving images that provoked a response. He had discovered a way to record his developing imagination.

LEAVING FOR AMERICA

Lee graduated in 1975 and was immediately required to fulfill his military service for three more years. Not much is known about his military career, but all soldiers at the time had to take an oath against the Communists, and most learned they had to be very careful about what they said and did. Taiwan still thought it might be attacked by China (many in the Chinese military favored an attack; some still do), and American military support continued to flow to Taiwan throughout the 1970s.

As soon as he got out, Lee made plans to go to the United States to continue his education in acting and film. For many students in Taiwan at the time, going to America was not only a possibility but a necessity for being considered serious and successful. Some Taiwanese women would not even date a man who had no plans to study in America, whose universities were considered among the best in the world. By the 1970s, the first generation of Taiwan-born children was leaving for the United States at a rate of 2,000 per year. So, on the recommendation of a friend, Lee applied to the undergraduate theater program at the University of Illinois. He told his father that he hoped to return to Taiwan as a professor. His father told him that he had better get a doctorate degree.

Partly because of the two short movies he had made at the academy, Lee was accepted to the university and came to the United States in the late summer of 1978. He was about to become truly multicultural. His life entered a whole new chapter.

3

Becoming Asian American, 1978–1990

Some Taiwanese had heard stories that America had streets paved with gold and impossibly tall skyscrapers with windows hardened by diamonds. Ang Lee knew many things about America, but it was only an abstract and vague knowledge from movies and books. He was now ready for the real thing. In August 1978, he touched down in the United States for the first time. He landed in Chicago and was driven to the University of Illinois Urbana-Champaign campus, so he now found himself in the middle of America.

Lee had been accepted into the College of Fine and Applied Arts as an undergraduate theater major. At 23, he was older than most undergraduates, but he still had to rely on his family for financial support. The Theater Department at the University of Illinois is one of the best in the world. In 1978, the Krannert Center for the Performing Arts was still new and had four separate theaters spread out over four acres. The university has had many famous arts and entertainment students besides Ang Lee—film critic Roger Ebert, comedian

Andy Richter, and *Playboy* magazine founder Hugh Hefner are just a few.

GETTING SHOCKED BY A CULTURE

Author Iris Chang, herself a graduate of the University of Illinois, captures two of the shocks Taiwanese students face right away in the United States in her landmark book *The Chinese in America*:

> American food repulsed them. Many Taiwanese Americans remember being half-starved through their first term.... They described the horrors of barbecues, college cafeterias, and inauthentic Chinese restaurants.... "The sight of a hot dog dripping with red tomato sauce and yellow mustard is enough to take your appetite away." ... And inevitably, the newcomers struggled with the language. At first most could not grasp the freewheeling American [speech]. Their studies back in Taiwan had not prepared them for the slang terms.... Jokes had incomprehensible punch lines. It was often difficult to follow the lectures of professors, to decipher certain passages in textbooks.

American-born theater students had spent their lives steeped in the English language. Facial expressions, gestures, and voice tone were also second nature. Lee told writer John Lahr, "I would take 10 hours to read a script that everyone else read in an hour.... I understood only about half of what was going on."

Notions that many take for granted were not easy for the new Taiwanese students. Some had trouble simply telling one Caucasian face from another. Chang writes that her mother said, "White people all looked alike to me in the beginning. Pale skin, big noses—that was all I could notice in the beginning." Some felt an immediate racism.

The United States was in an economic recession in the late 1970s and early 1980s, and some blamed Asians. One popular bumper sticker in the Detroit, Michigan, area read, "Unemployment—Made in Japan"—referring to auto-manufacturing jobs being lost to Japan. Vincent Chin, a Chinese engineering student in Michigan, was beaten to death with a baseball bat by two unemployed workers who mistook him for Japanese. Chinese-American activists organized to protest the light sentences the criminals received. Lee has never said he felt explicit racism, and indeed most Americans by the late 1970s had stopped using slurs to refer to Asians, but he was aware of being different in a strange land. Leaving one culture to live in a completely new one is never easy. It is almost always a shock.

FINDING A SOUL MATE

People, though, have a way of absorbing the shock of the new. Newcomers often make a strong connection to someone they meet very early on. Taking advantage of an informal but large network of Taiwanese-born students in the Urbana-Champaign area, Lee found himself in a car with other Taiwanese-American students within days of his arrival. They were traveling to watch the soon-to-be Little League world champions, the team from the Pinkuang Little League in Taipei, Taiwan. Lee told writer John Lahr that the people in the car "were doing science, agriculture, and medicine, and I was still a transfer undergrad in theater, which is almost laughable."

An attractive young woman sat next to him and began to talk. She seemed interested in hearing about him. She listened, and his natural shyness disappeared. "I never pursued a woman," Lee told Lahr. "I was a shy guy. . . . I couldn't find anybody to listen to me. And there she was, interested in what I did."

Her name was Jane Lin, and they began a lifelong relationship that lasts to this day—she would become his wife a few years later. Throughout his adult life she has been his emotional center, the one person who supported him in more ways than he could count.

Lin was an outgoing and independent graduate student in the fast-moving and complex field of microbiology. In her research, she would later explore how cells communicate with each other. Her intelligence was obvious to Lee, and soon he felt so comfortable with her that he could confide anything. They just connected, even though Lee was not the kind of man Lin's family would have chosen for her.

Lin told Lahr that, once Lee opened up to her, "he just talks, about everything. I fall asleep, I wake up, he's still talking." Lee could sit with her, his arms wrapped around her, and feel comforted. He found a warmth that had been missing in his adult life. He was no longer alone.

A STAGE ACTOR BECOMES A STAGE DIRECTOR

Lee found that his language problems were a big enough obstacle that he was not able to succeed as an actor, even though he had very much enjoyed performing and had come to the University of Illinois to get a degree in that field. His life quickly approached a second crisis, another defining moment. Fortunately, the university had a strong program in theater direction as well as acting, and Lee began to experiment with directing actors on stage.

His first experience as a student director was in a production of Eugene Ionesco's *The Chairs,* a disturbing play that focuses on an old man and an old woman following a great world disaster (the play was written soon after World War II). The play implies that the elderly couple are among the last people left on Earth, and they are arranging chairs for guests to hear a lecture from someone who has an important message to convey, a message that will change and even save the world. Unfortunately, the guests are imaginary, and the person delivering the message is deaf and mute. The old couple commit suicide. Not only does language fail, the play seems to be saying, but trying to make sense of things is impossible. In his program notes, Ionesco wrote: "As the world is incomprehensible to me, I am waiting for someone to explain it." For Lee, his new world must have seemed similarly incomprehensible.

He soon studied plays by Tennessee Williams, Harold Pinter, Bertolt Brecht, and Eugene O'Neill. These were all new to him. He later told journalists that "the look of Western theater struck me in a big way." He became quite adept at understanding stage direction, setting up scenes and arranging actors within those scenes, a practice known as "blocking." Many feel that stage direction is an ideal preparation for film direction, just as stage acting can be perfect training for film actors. A stage director cannot zoom the audience in and out of the action as a film director can, but both stage directors and film directors block out actor positions scene by scene. They have to know what is central and what isn't, what to put in and what to leave out.

In 1980, Lee graduated from the University of Illinois with a B.F.A., a bachelor of fine arts degree in theater/theater direction. The road to that degree, however, had been difficult, and even though he loved the theater, he wanted and needed to express himself some other way. Lee came to a third defining moment in his life. He knew that stage directors had little to do after opening night; the actors were the center of the theater. He also knew from his short film work at the Taiwan Academy of Arts that film directors did not have the limitations of stage directors and that they could do a lot after filming was over. He decided to take on the next biggest challenge he could find—film direction.

MOVING FROM STAGE TO FILM

He used the same two short films he had made as a student in Taipei to apply for graduate studies in film at New York University (NYU), another very prestigious university with an even longer history of success in the arts and entertainment field. Lee was accepted into the Tisch School of the Arts at NYU as a master's degree candidate in film production. He now moved to the epicenter of American cultural life, where he would make the transition from stage to screen.

He learned by doing. He also had to unlearn by doing. He told reporter Ann Hornaday that, at NYU, "I spent three or four years learning to forget about theater."

He learned that a stage actor uses his or her voice and whole body movements to carry much of the acting, but a film actor uses facial expressions much more. In film, the human face during a close-up camera shot is almost 100 times larger than an actual face. The human face carries a film while the human voice carries a play.

Lee at first helped other students make their films. He noticed something right away: Even though his English was not fluent, people began to listen to him as he did the lighting or recorded the sound. One student he helped was Spike Lee, two years ahead of him at NYU. Ang Lee used to joke that they were brothers (Spike Lee is African American). Spike Lee's master's thesis movie was *Joe's Bed-Stuy Barbershop: We Cut Heads,* and Lee learned some invaluable lessons as assistant cameraman during its making. Ang Lee later told movie museum curator David Schwartz that "I got to see how he [Spike Lee] makes movies and all that. That's how the school works out: We help each other." Spike Lee would soon go on to make *She's Gotta Have It,* which was released in wide circulation and was a commercial success. Ang Lee was inspired—someone recently out of film school at NYU could make it big.

Next, Lee made several short student films of his own, including *The Runner, Beat the Artist,* and *Shades of the Lake.* These films were good enough to win him a full scholarship; he no longer had to rely on his family's financial support. His master's thesis was a 43-minute movie called *Fine Line.* It captured the love and cultural tensions that existed between a Chinese girl, Piu Piu, and a tough Italian boy, Mario. It was mainly filmed in two New York City "villages": Chinatown and Little Italy. Lee cast an unknown acting student named Chazz Palminteri, who

Spike Lee is shown with actress Tracy Camilla Johns during a release party for his 1986 film *She's Gotta Have It*. Ang Lee worked as an assistant cameraman when Spike Lee was making his master's thesis film at New York University's film school. Ang Lee would not have the same early success that Spike Lee had after graduating.

SPIKE LEE

One of the most famous and controversial film directors to graduate from the NYU film school is Shelton Lee, better known as "Spike." Lee graduated with a master's degree in 1982, two years ahead of Ang Lee.

Spike Lee's first movie after leaving NYU was *She's Gotta Have It*, shot in two weeks with a budget of $160,000. It made more than $7 million, attracting a diverse audience interested in its story of race relations and urban life. He also played a character in the movie named Mars Blackmon, a young man fascinated with basketball player Michael Jordan. When Nike executives saw the film, they signed Lee to direct a commercial featuring Lee as Mars Blackmon and Michael Jordan as himself, to promote the "Air Jordan" sneaker. The result was a classic and effective campaign for Air Jordans.

His movies *Do the Right Thing* and *4 Little Girls* received Academy Award nominations, and his *Mo' Better Blues* and *Jungle Fever* are famous and successful explorations of self-discovery amid racial and urban tensions.

Lee has also been at the center of several controversies. One occurred at the 1998 Cannes Film Festival in France. After a screening of his movie *Summer of Sam*, Lee was asked if violent American movies and television were the causes of America's high rates of crime. He replied that the number of guns in America was a bigger problem and joked that the head of the National Rifle Association, former actor Charlton Heston, should be shot. He reiterated that he was kidding and did not want to see his name in the headlines the next day saying he wanted Heston shot. In fact, that was exactly what happened in newspapers and news outlets around the world.

Lee's public controversies also serve to bring more attention to his important work. *When the Levees Broke*, his four-hour television documentary on New Orleans after Hurricane Katrina, captured the devastation, pain, and loss there in vivid images and stories.

would later receive an Academy Award nomination for his role in *Bullets Over Broadway.*

A MARRIAGE MADE IN NEW YORK

In 1983, while Lee was working on *Fine Line,* his parents decided to make their first visit to the United States. Lee's father had just retired, and his parents were determined to see more of the world, just as their son was doing. It is also possible they missed their son and wanted to see him after five years apart.

Lee and Jane Lin had maintained a long-distance relationship while she continued her Ph.D. work and research at the University of Illinois. Lee decided he would ask Lin to marry him while his parents were in the United States. The Chinese have a symbol for "double happiness" used at weddings, and having his parents and Lin together would be a double happiness for him. Lin accepted his proposal and came to New York. Her mother was not happy. Lin told John Lahr that her mother said, "Why did you pick this one, with all the other nice boys around—engineering and regular people?" Lin replied: "I earn my own living. I can choose whoever I want." To go against the wishes of her mother took courage, and a willingness to follow her desires showed that Lin had a surprisingly romantic streak. Lee would join a cast of millions with mother-in-law problems.

Lee and Lin exchanged marriage vows in New York City at a City Hall civil ceremony. Lee's mother was embarrassed at how fast and unplanned the whole scene was. But they all went to a nearby reception banquet where everyone celebrated with a vengeance. Family tensions needed to be released. The families would later learn that Lee and Lin conceived their first child that night.

The honeymoon that followed had elements of a family comedy. Lee told reporter Ann Hornaday, "Then we had six people on the honeymoon—us, my parents, Jane's father, and her sister. It was harder than making a movie. At least when I make a movie, everyone listens to me." The wedding and honeymoon would become raw material for scenes in his movies.

The marriage would be difficult at first: Lin was still several years away from getting her Ph.D. and had to return immediately to Urbana-Champaign. Lee had to finish his master's thesis film. In fact, when their first son, Haan, was born in 1984, Lin did not even tell Lee about the delivery. She had never held a child before, and she now had to balance raising that child along with her studies. They were married, but they both struggled, their careers and fiercely independent temperaments keeping them apart.

WINNING HIS FIRST "BEST DIRECTOR" AWARD

Lee finished *Fine Line* and graduated from NYU in 1984 with an M.F.A. (master of fine arts) in film production. He had become one of the school's top film students. Lee faced yet another important decision. Should he move back to Urbana-Champaign to be with his wife and child? Would there be any chances to make movies there? Should he go back to Taiwan and make feature-length movies and wait for Jane to get her degree and join him? Should he stay in New York? He was torn.

He decided to return to Taiwan. But he waited until *Fine Line* was entered into the 1985 NYU Film Festival and shown to an important audience of critics, Hollywood executives, and agents—the NYU film school is closely watched by people looking for directing talent. Lee and *Fine Line* won "Best Director" and "Best Film," so he soon got a call he would never forget. At 9:30 P.M. the night before he was to leave for Taiwan, as he was packing, someone from NYU told him that an agent from the William Morris agency had been looking for him. Lee did not know who William Morris was. But he learned that it was one of the world's largest talent agencies, and an agent wanted to sign him on as a client to make movies in the United States. Lee later told Hornaday, "I didn't have a choice. I just wanted to make my way into the system." One of the biggest decisions of his life had been made for him.

A FAMILY REUNITED

In January 1986, Jane Lin got her Ph.D. in microbiology from the University of Illinois, and the family was reunited. Finally, Lee could be with his wife and son Haan, now two years old. He would now be a real father.

They first moved into a room in a house owned by a friend in Chappaqua, New York, a town later made famous as the home of Bill and Hillary Clinton. The room was a bit cold, however, and the friends did not have children, so Lee and Lin were afraid they were being disruptive. Lin told John Lahr, "We felt trapped." They then moved into an apartment in White Plains, which is closer to New York City. It was the first floor of a two-story house, roughly 800 square feet (74 square meters) of living space. They all slept in one bedroom. It would be their home for the next 11 years.

They lived in an interesting and historic area: They had a cluster of trees behind their house, and George Washington had once stayed in a farmhouse nearby. Lin told Lahr, "We had a very simple life. We were happy about little things." The family took outings to Rockefeller State Park Preserve and spent a good deal of time at the White Plains Public Library. Lee's favorite place to eat was Kentucky Fried Chicken.

Lin got a job as a researcher at a laboratory in Valhalla, New York, and Lee tried to find work in the movie business. He started at the bottom, with his William Morris agent getting him a job as a production assistant (PA). PAs work either in an office or on a movie set, making copies of scripts, answering phones, getting lunch, and setting up appointments. It is exhausting and low-paying work. For Lee, those jobs would come and go, none of them steady.

When he was not working, he did have time to play with his son, cook for the family (Lin did not like to cook), and be a househusband. And he also had time to think and write movie scripts.

Lee found it hard to get to the next step in the system, beyond a PA. He was coming up with ideas for movies and writing scripts, but no one was buying them. He was not getting noticed. He told David Schwartz:

> Each time I thought of something exciting, I'd call up [my] agent. [He'd say,] "There must be, like, five such ideas being written. And two of them are in production." . . . And I go through the ordeal of pitching [trying to sell a script or a movie idea]. . . . [You] write for months, then pitch; then there'd be a few people who'd be interested . . . [then] it would gradually die down. And then the next one would come up.

Lee told writer Jennifer Frey of *The New York Times,* "I sent in script after script . . . there would be interest, I'd rewrite, hurry up, turn it in, and wait weeks and weeks." Hundreds of scripts were turned down, even though Julia Roberts was briefly interested in one project and Italian actor Giancarlo Giannini in another. Rejection flattened but did not defeat Lee.

SURVIVING AND USING SIX YEARS OF REJECTION

The months of not getting a script bought or a movie idea produced turned into years. Lee did not improve as a "pitcher" of his projects. When trying to sell himself and his ideas or scripts to film executives, Lee tended either to try to act out parts or not say much. When he did talk, he often did not get to the point right away, which Hollywood executives are famous for insisting on. His three-minute pitches would stretch into a half-hour. He was a terrible salesman. He was still not fluent in English, and some executives even suggested that he take a Berlitz course to improve his speaking. Lee told Lahr, "Being a foreigner, you look dumber, your speech is slower. People who have a lot of money to throw around, they feel unconfident because you don't look confident. I just wasn't American enough." He seems to have suffered a crisis of confidence, seeing himself as he thought others saw him. He seemed too Chinese to be American and too American to be Chinese. He was often feeling, as he would later say, trapped between cultures, not belonging to either. He was an outsider once again.

This period in his life took an emotional toll on the whole family. Lin told John Lahr, "All those sleepless nights. For a long time I thought that was how we would be for the rest of our lives. He's just going to talk about these things, and a movie's never going to be made." Lee described this period as "the toughest time for Jane and me. She didn't know what a film career was like, and neither did I." He even took up tennis, not so much for the love of the game but as a distraction. He told London journalist Liese Spencer that, when he played tennis, "I didn't want to play the game. I just wanted to hit something."

Most articles about Lee's life, and Lee himself, call this time his "development hell," a period of frustration alternating with boredom. But new research on creativity and success, as described in Malcolm Gladwell's *Outliers: The Story of Success*, suggests that, for someone to get very good at what they do, they often need to invest roughly 10,000 hours into doing it. Gladwell points to Microsoft's Bill Gates, who at 13 was granted access to a high school computer for roughly 10,000 hours and taught himself programming. The Beatles played together in Europe for almost 10,000 hours from 1960 to 1964 before they became rock music's ultimate success story.

Lee's six years of development, at 35 hours per week, translates into roughly 10,000 hours. These were not wasted years.

They were the years he formed his ideas, learned more about the culture of America and Hollywood, and created a kind of mental database about making movies. He sowed the seeds of creativity that would develop later. Lee told NPR's Scott Simon, "I learned a lot about what a feature-length movie needs just through the exercise of writing scripts." He almost certainly learned the hard way how to construct a basic script: decide on a theme and key characters, move those characters toward or away from their goals, build in conflict, and resolve the conflict.

Gladwell points to another element of creative success. Some people are late bloomers, and Lee was surely one of them. Gladwell writes:

> Late bloomers' stories are invariably love stories.... We'd like to think that mundane matters like loyalty, steadfastness, and the willingness to keep writing checks to support what looks like failure have nothing to do with something as rarefied as genius. But sometimes genius is anything but rarefied: Sometimes it's just the thing that emerges after . . . years of working at the kitchen table.

Lee did work for years at and near the kitchen table in the White Plains apartment, and he did have someone who showed him steadfast loyalty and support—his wife. Gladwell also notes that late bloomers often have conflicted personalities and need a period to "ferment." They look like failures. For them, learning is more important than anything, and they need time to learn. Another late bloomer, painter Paul Cézanne, was famous for painting, then repainting again and again, slashing canvases in fits of frustration. Writer Mark Twain took almost 10 years to write *Huckleberry Finn* because he was experimenting with mixing genres and plot lines.

In January 1991, Ang Lee met James Schamus, the man who would become his collaborator and his good friend. Just before the meeting, Lee had received financing from the Central Motion Picture Corporation in Taiwan to make his first feature film.

Lin decided that she valued her husband not for what he did or what he was going to become, but for who he was. They lived mostly off her salary for six long years, but she never gave up on him. In 1990, they had a second child, Mason. Lee had $23 in his bank account—his total life savings. He was 36.

GOVERNMENT AND A NEW BEST FRIEND TO THE RESCUE

The government of Taiwan believed in the importance of the arts, especially the importance of film. The government felt that it had a role in supporting a moviemaking industry that, by the late 1980s, was losing jobs to film companies based in Hong Kong. For years, the Taiwanese government awarded a $16,000 prize annually to the best screenplay by a Taiwanese citizen. Lee had written many screenplays, so he thought he had nothing to lose by sending in several. He was still not a U.S. citizen (he has only recently become one), so he qualified.

Just as he had reached rock bottom in his confidence in himself and his talent, his fortunes changed overnight, thanks to his government (even though he had not been in Taiwan for 12 years). He not only won the 1990 award for best screenplay, he won second place as well. First place went to his script *Pushing Hands* (which he had recently finished), and second place went to *The Wedding Banquet* (which he had written years before, after his own wedding). It must have seemed like a miracle. It was certainly one of the best examples of double happiness in his life.

Then, he was blessed with triple happiness. The government-funded Central Motion Picture Corporation (CMPC) in Taiwan agreed to pay $400,000 toward the making of a movie based on the screenplay *Pushing Hands*. CMPC had funded several low-budget movies about family relationships directed by inexperienced filmmakers. Lee fit that profile.

Inspired by the award, and armed with some promised money, Lee walked into the offices of a very small American movie production company in New York, called Good Machine, in January 1991. The company had just been formed by two very creative and talented young men, Ted Hope and James Schamus. They wanted to find young directors and help them get movies made. Lee met the man, James Schamus, who would serve as his guide, his translator, his negotiator, and eventually his best friend. Lee would never be poor and out of work again.

4
Finally Making Movies, 1991–1994

Good Machine at first consisted of a desk and two chairs in a building in Lower Manhattan. Ted Hope and James Schamus jokingly called their new company the "king of no-budget filmmaking." John Lahr recounted what happened when Lee walked through the door at Good Machine in 1991:

> The first thing Lee said was, "If I don't make a movie soon, I think I'll die." "It was clear when Ang left the room why he had not made a movie in six years," Schamus says. "The idea of flying this guy to Los Angeles for a story meeting—forget it. When he left the office, I turned to Ted and said two things. One was, 'Boy, this guy can't pitch his way out of a paper bag.' And two: 'He wasn't pitching a movie, he was describing a movie he'd already made. He just needs somebody to realize it. . . . This guy's a filmmaker.'"

With Lee's funding for *Pushing Hands,* work began with Schamus and Good Machine on how to turn the script into a film. When Lee wrote the script, he was writing a story that he never realized he would have to film. He told *New York Times* journalist Peter Nichols, "I was sitting home alone, cooking, getting bored and spaced out. So to nurture my spirit, I conjured a story of an old man, a *tai chi* master." The story is about a Chinese grandfather living in the suburbs of New York City with his Chinese-born son, his American daughter-in-law, and his grandson. Master Chu (the grandfather) was a *tai chi* teacher in Beijing before coming to America. *Tai chi* is an ancient Chinese martial art with training techniques that have been adapted all over the world. It can help with balance, blood circulation, and overall fitness. "Pushing hands" is usually a two-person technique that uses the physical tension between the two people after they have locked their straightened arms. Each tries to balance himself while unbalancing the other. The metaphor for two cultures and generations pushing and pulling each other is very visual.

Master Chu struggles with the tensions and differences he feels as an outsider in America. He speaks little English, and his daughter-in-law speaks even less Chinese. Their relationship has many misunderstandings and resentments as they shout at each other in different languages, but there's some humor as well. Finally, Master Chu moves out of their house into Chinatown, leaving a note that says in China they were happy with very few material things, and in America they are unhappy with a great deal of material things. Chu gets a job as a dishwasher but is fired for washing too slowly. His pride gets him into some trouble, and he even ends up in jail. He eventually is able to use his *tai chi* skills to survive and becomes a teacher. Each of the three main characters makes compromises, and the story has a happy but realistic ending.

Actors Sihung Lung *(left)* and Bo Z. Wang appear in a scene from *Pushing Hands*, Ang Lee's directorial debut. Lung played Master Chu, a *tai chi* teacher from China who was living in the United States with his son (Wang) and his American daughter-in-law. With its themes of Chinese and American cultures clashing, the film was a big success in Taiwan.

LEE'S FIRST FEATURE FILM SHOOT

On the first day of filming in New York City, Lee gathered the cast and crew and began a good-luck ritual he still performs with every film shoot: He brought in flowers, sticks of incense, bowls of uncooked rice, and a gong, and made a brief speech.

Since the budget provided only 24 working days of filming, the actors had to rehearse many times before shooting a scene. There was no time or money for expensive retakes. Lee had chosen an assistant director from Taipei named Chou

THE PLAYERS IN MOVIEMAKING

A movie often begins with one person's idea. Transforming that idea onto the screen, though, takes many people, sometimes more than 1,000. Many people in the film industry are very creative, and some are extremely business-smart. A few are both, and they tend to rise to the top of the industry.

The producer of a movie is a major player. He or she usually hires or fires the other major player, the director. Standard practice in Hollywood is that the producer handles the business side (hiring the director and the film crew, getting investors, arranging for a distributor of the film) and the director handles the artistic side (controlling who and what is filmed, and what gets shown in the final movie). But their roles mix, depending on the people and the project. The simplest description of the two players is that the producer gets the director what he or she needs to make the film and the director makes a film the producer wants.

A film truism is that neither directors nor producers think they get all the credit they deserve. Another truism is that for the first half of the twentieth century the producer was king, and for the second half the director was. Recent blockbuster franchises like James Bond movies and sequels to *Spider-Man* and *Batman* tend to put more power back in the hands of producers, since the director becomes less important when a brand-name movie series already exists.

Making a film is a highly collaborative effort. Other important players are the scriptwriters, actors, distributors and marketers who get the film shown in theaters, cinematographers who actually do the filming, art directors, editors who cut down the raw footage into a film, musical composers who make or find the right music, and sound engineers. Depending on the movie, wardrobe/costume designers, computer and visual effects designers, make-up/hair designers, and the lighting directors also become important.

Hsu-wei, and she noticed that the filming took a toll on Lee, turning some of his hair gray. She wrote in a blog that Lee is "simple and straightforward in the way he deals with people. . . . He's one whose spirit is quite like an ancient Chinese scholar."

Lee felt his way through the filming process, to see how assertive he should be with the actors and the crew, or how relaxed. Film directors are usually either "hands-on" or "hands-off" with their actors. Hands-on directors like to control exactly what the actors are doing, and hands-off directors let the actors figure out a good deal for themselves. Lee is both, depending on the actor. He both pushed and pulled.

Pushing Hands was very popular in Taiwan. Its themes of Chinese and American cultures clashing within a divided family are still relevant today. Many Taiwanese film fans say it is their favorite Ang Lee movie. The movie was a success with Taiwanese critics as well. It was nominated for eight 1991 Golden Horse awards (Taiwan's equivalent of the Oscars) and won three. It was an impressive start. New directors do not usually get a second chance unless they earn it.

PLANNING *THE WEDDING BANQUET*

Lee's second-place script in the Taiwan government competition, *The Wedding Banquet,* now got financing for even more money than the first. The Central Motion Picture Corporation in Taiwan wanted the movie made in six weeks and provided a budget of $750,000.

The *Wedding Banquet* script is based on a true story about a gay Taiwanese immigrant living in New York City with his partner. Wai-Tung Gao is almost 30 years old, and his Taiwanese parents (who do not know he is gay) are eager for him to marry and have children. They hire a dating service, but to stall for time Wai-Tung tells the service that his date must be an opera singer with at least two Ph.D.s who speaks five languages. To his amazement, the dating service finds such a person, a wonderfully comic sequence. He decides to marry a poor Mainland Chinese woman living in New York, Wei-Wei, so she can get her "green card," her official approval to stay in the United States. His parents arrive in America to plan and attend his wedding and banquet. Wei-Wei seduces the drunken Wai-Tung after the banquet and becomes pregnant. The story eventually has a happy ending for all.

Lee told interviewer Richard Mowe that the movie continued his exploration of family dramas. "I'm not gay, but in the movie the son's homosexuality poses the ultimate challenge to parental traditions and older values, which is a dramatized version of how I felt about my upbringing."

Ang Lee continued to explore clashing cultures with his second film, *The Wedding Banquet*, which was released in 1993. The cast included *(from left)* May Chin as Wei-Wei, Ah Lei Gua as Mrs. Gao, Mitchell Lichtenstein as Simon, Sihung Lung as Mr. Gao, and Winston Chao as Wai-Tung Gao.

Lee always thought casting was crucial to the success of a movie. David Lee, one of the production assistants on the movie, tells the story of how far Lee was willing to go to get just the right actor. There is one small part in *The Wedding Banquet* for a wealthy older woman, and Lee and others auditioned more than 100 women. Finally, a Mrs. Kuan from upstate New York was brought to Lee, who knew immediately that she was perfect for the role. She appears for a few seconds in one scene.

One of the director's jobs is to simply solve problems. Lee did this in many ways during the shooting. When a woman was not working out well on the filming team, he arranged for her to be reassigned to a job taking advantage of her strengths. When some on the team objected to the hectic pace and round-the-clock filming, he agreed to pay them from his director's fee.

The movie was released on August 4, 1993, his first film to hit American theaters (*Pushing Hands* was not released in the United States until 1994.) When the film's distributor called Lee to arrange for a limousine to take him to the New York opening, Lee was asked what kind of liquor he wanted in the limo bar. Lee replied that he did not want any liquor and that a regular car would be enough. He did not need or want a stretch limo. Lee waited outside an early screening in Greenwich Village. He heard the rousing laughter of the audience and saw people happily discussing the movie as they left. He found himself in tears.

The movie was an international success. He said years later in an interview for the Museum of the Moving Image, "That's the first time I tasted a hit. Not only a hit in Taiwan, but an international hit. Things really started to take off." *The Wedding Banquet* earned more than $30 million, which made it the most profitable (most dollars earned per dollar spent on production) movie of 1993. It was even more profitable than another movie that year, *Jurassic Park. The Wedding Banquet* was nominated for an Oscar, for "Best Foreign-Language

Film." It was the first time a Taiwanese-born director had been nominated. And it won the Berlin Film Festival's Golden Bear award, Germany's equivalent of the Academy Award. That award, Lee would later say to entertainment reporters, finally made an impression on his father. Perhaps his son was going to be a success after all.

THE THIRD MOVIE IS THE CHARM

When a director has a hit, the scripts begin to flow. Lee remembers that he received many scripts, most of which were heartwarming family comedies. He told journalist Steven Rea that he now wanted to "lay back a little bit. I want to avoid becoming the flavor of the month." But Lee is always restless; lying back between films just was not possible early in his career. There was too much to do after doing nothing for so long. He completed work on *The Wedding Banquet* on December 23, 1992, and the next day flew to Taiwan to scout his next project. He missed Christmas with his family.

Lee and Schamus had written a script called *Eat Drink Man Woman*. The story is about a master chef named Chu living in Taipei who has lost his beloved wife and has three very different daughters he must raise by himself. Each daughter is struggling with a problem. The oldest, Jia-Jen, is more traditional than her surroundings in modern Taipei. The middle daughter, Jia-Chien, wants to be a chef like her father but is not permitted to do so. The youngest daughter, Jia-Ning, works at Wendy's and gets pregnant without being married. Chu finds it hard to communicate with his daughters, and the daughters find it difficult to communicate with one another and with their father. But they show their love indirectly through elaborate Sunday feasts. Chu surprises his daughters by marrying a much younger friend. He liberates himself and proves to be the most "modern" character in the movie.

This time, Lee wanted to shoot the movie in Taipei, not in New York. He hoped to be a full-fledged Chinese filmmaker, not just an American one. He had a budget of $1.5 million, twice as much as his previous picture. He knew who he wanted in the leading role of Chu—the same experienced actor he had in his first two films, Sihung Lung.

Lee had to hire three of Taiwan's most accomplished chefs to create the food for the lavish meals. The movie opens with four minutes of their wizardry: chopping vegetables, preparing sea bass, making lotus flower soup. More than 100 recipes were used in the film. The opening four minutes took eight days of filming. One shot of tofu being chopped required six hours to film. Lee told journalist Steven Rea, "From a production standpoint, the food was more difficult to work with than any actor. . . . In order to capture the food as it was being prepared, and then as it was served, still steaming, we had to figure new ways to light it. We'd do it over and over again."

Lee described his role as director:

> It [*Eat Drink Man Woman*] is my homecoming movie. . . . In Taiwan, it's much more of a director's show. Here [in America], it's the producer who runs the production and the director pretty much makes artistic decisions. In Taiwan, you have to generate everything, initiate everything. People look to the director for everything. . . . There's a different working philosophy which takes 10 times the director's energy.

In Taiwan, he was king, not president. He had local people follow him, offering tea and cigars. They expected him to shout and carry on, so he did. He told journalist Richard Mowe, "I am a nice guy, so it was very hard for me to yell, but once I did it felt good."

A THREE-HIT WONDER

When he finished filming in December 1993, he flew home from Taiwan, eager to spend New Year's with his family. He had missed Christmas with them for the second year in a row. After he landed on a cold, late-December night feeling sick, he was delighted to see the lights on in his White Plains home. Jane and the boys rushed to welcome him after the long shoot. Even though he had months of film editing ahead of him in

Being Asian American

TWO VERY DIFFERENT WORLDVIEWS

Ang Lee and his main characters are often grappling with what it means to be both an Asian and an American. Lee, especially in his first three movies, worked though many issues about his dual heritage. He fully explored the difficulties a Chinese speaker faces in America. Biographer Whitney Dilley writes, "The early films of Ang Lee chart a course into the dense and treacherous territory of the Chinese speaker approaching Western culture through English as a second language."

Lee summarized his Asian influences in a conversation with John Lahr, who wrote:

Western drama is built on the escalation of tension; Chinese life is built around the reduction of it. Lee is a curious amalgam of both influences. . . . "In Chinese culture, the only way to rise above your class is through study," Lee says. . . . "In my [Chinese] culture, you're part of the group. You have to find harmony, so you repress, repress, repress. So far, repression is my biggest source of creativity. Repression—release. . . . That's a good story."

Being Asian American may mean having to reconcile two very different views on some significant matters. For example,

New York at Good Machine, he could be home at night with his family.

Eat Drink Man Woman was released on August 3, 1994, and was yet another international hit, even bigger than *The Wedding Banquet*. It was also nominated for an Oscar for "Best Foreign-Language Film," and won many other awards. Lee had reached a milestone. He had completed what he called his "Father Knows Best" trilogy of movies (the reference is to a 1950s American

many Asians do not feel that they are protected by a supreme being with some human qualities; "God" is more like a force of nature. Americans and Asians may feel good and bad in different ways. Many Americans may believe in some version of "original sin," that to be human is to be deeply flawed. Americans may be exposed to the seven vices and seven virtues, while many Asians have been educated in the seven passions (joy, anger, sorrow, fear, love, lust, and hate). Americans may look for elation and "peak experiences" in being happy, while Asians may seek tranquil joy. Americans may see a world made of unconnected things, where Asians may see a world of interlocking forces.

To be Asian American is to try to mesh the two different worldviews, perhaps to accept that both elation and tranquil joy are a part of life, or that passions lead to both vices and virtues.

An Asian American may try to combine the respect for community with the need to be independent. Many Asian Americans try to cultivate a dual nature, but some feel they are neither Asian nor American. They may feel like citizens of the world, moving more freely from culture to culture and using what they need from each.

television show in which the father's authority was recognized). The father in each is a key figure, and he doesn't always know best. But he knows enough, and what he doesn't know, he tries to learn.

Each movie also taught Lee many aspects of moviemaking. He now knew how to build tension in a movie and release it. He found that the more you respect and support members of the film crew, the harder they work. He was learning how to frame scenes and move actors around, discovering what to put in and what to leave out of a frame.

Lee was now a success as a director, a three-hit wonder. Each movie had more box-office and critical success than the one before. He was now moving to the next big challenge: dealing with a major studio and real movie stars, something he had avoided so far. He was ready for Hollywood.

5

Becoming Westernized, 1995–1999

Emma Thompson is a famous and accomplished English actor. She had an early fascination with writer Jane Austen's work and had written a screenplay based on the Austen novel *Sense and Sensibility*. She had waited for years for the right director to make this film. She was watching *Eat Drink Man Woman* one evening and gasped when she saw a scene with two of the sisters talking to each other; the older one says, "What do you know of my heart?" Thompson had written exactly the same line in her screenplay. She knew this was not just coincidence; this film was made by a director who knew family drama.

Thompson and producer Lindsay Doran sent Ang Lee the *Sense and Sensibility* script, and he thought they had made a mistake. He did not know who Jane Austen was. He told journalist Michael Warren, "I read the script about halfway, and I thought, 'They're crazy, what do I know about nineteenth-century England?'" But Thompson and Doran finally persuaded him to direct the movie. They told Warren, "Forget about the fact that he's [Lee] only made movies that are mostly in Chinese. This kind of strict social code that dictates what people can and can't say and do is so much more familiar to him growing up in twentieth-century Taiwan than it would be to people in America or Britain."

Sense and Sensibility has many plot lines, but the major one concerns two sisters, Elinor and Marianne Dashwood. Elinor is the older sister, practical, sensible, and wise beyond her years. Marianne is younger and filled with sensibility—passionate and romantic emotions. Eventually, after many complications, the sensible and practical sister finds her true love, Edward Ferrars. Marianne ends up loving and marrying Colonel Brandon, a practical choice. This occurs after she is hurt by the dashing and handsome Mr. Willoughby, who is not honest with her. Each sister has found something within—Elinor has found her sensibility, and Marianne has found sense.

Columbia Pictures gave Lee (and the producers) a $16 million budget to make the movie, a much larger amount than he ever had. He could afford elaborate ballroom scenes in wonderful British ancestral mansions in Devon, Somerset, and London, hundreds of extras, and real movie stars. Lee told journalist Liese Spencer, "Before I made Sense and Sensibility, I didn't have to worry about how people looked. Then I suddenly had to deal with movie stars."

MAKING SENSE AND SENSIBILITY

Lee cast Emma Thompson as Elinor, a relative unknown named Kate Winslet as Marianne, and the very popular Hugh Grant as Edward Ferrars. Alan Rickman, of Die Hard and Robin Hood fame, rounded out the leading cast as Colonel Brandon. This was a high-powered cast.

Just before leaving for England to begin filming Sense and Sensibility, Lee did something he always did before a long trip.

He made dozens of meals, including hundreds of dumplings, for his family and put them in the freezer—a month's worth of food. Cooking always relaxed him and gave him a way to show love.

At first, Lee had difficulties managing his all-star cast. He was used to being in charge, but these actors were accustomed to making contributions and suggestions. For example, on the first day of shooting, the characters played by Grant and Thompson meet for the first time, and Lee wanted the shot to be from far away, to show their garden setting and the distance between them. Grant and Thompson suggested a different shot,

Emma Thompson *(left)* and Kate Winslet starred in *Sense and Sensibility* (1995) as sisters Elinor and Marianne Dashwood. The film marked Ang Lee's first time directing established movie stars, and its $16 million budget was much higher than he had for any of his previous movies.

closer to them. Lee ended up losing sleep that night because he felt his authority was being undermined.

He told Warren: "What they're [the actors] used to is very stagy, very English tradition. . . . They feel they have to carry the movie. It's the Chinese nature to step back and let the picture tell the story." Lee wanted them to focus more on body language than words. He also had to tone down Grant's performance. Lee called Grant "a show-stealer." And, as always, Lee was willing to ask actors to do many takes to get a shot just right. When Winslet's character breathlessly meets the handsome Willoughby during a rainstorm, Winslet actually passed out from hyperventilation after being blasted by rain machines for some 50 takes.

Grant had a few nicknames for Lee, as described in John Lahr's work on Lee:

> "Ang would always come up to you and say something unexpectedly crushing," recalls Thompson, whom Lee urged not to "look so old." His first note to Kate Winslet . . . was "You will do better." Hugh Grant . . . nicknamed him Fang and, later, the Brute. At the wrap party [given after filming is over] Winslet and Thompson and other cast members rewrote the Rolling Stones' song "Angie" and serenaded their director: "Ang Lee/I still love you/ Remember all those nights we cried."

Thompson and the producers were delighted with the result. The film was beautiful—Lee had woven more English landscape into the movie than anyone thought possible. The actors gave wonderful performances, and the movie's pacing was slow enough to showcase the actors and yet fast enough to tell the story. Most movies have a pace that cuts to a new camera angle or shot every five seconds or so. Lee made one scene with Grant and Thompson that was more than four minutes long, almost unheard of. In the DVD extra scenes, Lee said that "good actors hang onto the screen" and fewer camera-angle changes are needed. These actors hung onto the screen.

THE STEPS OF MOVIEMAKING

Moviemakers usually divide the process of their art into three steps: preproduction, shooting, and postproduction. Preproduction is the time for writing a script, getting the financing together, hiring actors and crew, finding film locations, and planning the filming. Some directors "design" the film at this stage; famous director Alfred Hitchcock said that preproduction was the most important step and that the other two stages were relatively boring to him.

The filming itself is the next step, and the third step, postproduction, is considered to be the most important by Ang Lee. Lee has often said that filming a movie is like shopping for groceries and that the postproduction work is like doing the cooking.

A film is a series of shots, which is a single piece of film without breaks in the action. A shot may last 1/24 of a second (one frame of film) or 10 minutes (the amount of film a camera holds) or any length in between. Each shot must be spliced to the shots that come before and after it. The average two-hour film contains 500 to 1,000 shots fastened together. Most directors film several takes of a shot and decide later which is the best.

The person who first decides which takes of which shots are used is the film editor, along with the director. Lee has used the same film editor for virtually every movie—Tim Squyres. Squyres told *New York Times* journalist Bernice Napach that "at first a film is just a lot of footage. An editor assembles the pieces and then constructs the movie." Typically, Squyres will take about 70 hours of film footage to make the "first cut" of a two-hour movie. Then, Squyres and Lee work together for the "director's cut," often for 12 to 14 hours a day 6 days a week during postproduction, a process that usually lasts longer than the filming itself.

Lee was changed by the filming. He became more verbal, more willing to express his own sensibility. James Schamus told Warren that, by the end of the shoot, "Ang was starting to verbalize in a way that wasn't ever part of his world."

After a long and complicated postproduction, *Sense and Sensibility* was released on December 13, 1995, just in time for the holiday movie season. It was a box-office success, and the critics approved as well. The film won a Golden Globe for best drama. Emma Thompson, too, won a Golden Globe for her screenplay and thanked Lee warmly in her acceptance speech, saying he knew Jane Austen better than she did. It was high praise. He had captured on film a culture that was completely foreign to him, and he was ready now to capture another foreign world.

FINDING DISTURBIA

Lee always wants new challenges, and his next movie took on an entirely new look and feel. Schamus had enjoyed a book called *The Ice Storm*, by Rick Moody, about two families in New Canaan, Connecticut, in 1973, a rich town in a rich state. The two families were being torn apart as the parents gave in to the siren song of "open marriage" (in which spouses feel they do not have to be faithful to each other). The time of the novel was crucial—in 1973, the unpopular Vietnam War was still going on, the unpopular President Richard Nixon was declaring he was not a crook, and a gas shortage would trigger an economic crisis. America itself was in turmoil, as were the families.

Schamus sent the book to Lee, who immediately saw a movie possibility. He was fascinated by how different America in the early 1970s was from Taiwan at the same time. He told Laura Winters, "In the '50s, values were still conservative—family, success, stability. And then there was the romantic, rebellious '60s. [In the 1970s] the whole nation was going through a loss of innocence. It was a coming of age, even more so for the parents than for the kids." So, Schamus developed a script from the novel.

The two families in the script are the Hoods and the Carvers. Paul Hood, the teenage son of Elena and Ben Hood, comes home from his prep school for Thanksgiving vacation. He and his sister, Wendy, have trouble communicating with their parents and both are rebelling in quiet ways—experimenting with sex, alcohol, and drugs. Their parents are also having trouble: Ben is having an affair with neighbor Janey Carver, and Elena is depressed and unsure of where her life is going. Jim Carver is rarely home, and his two sons seem surprised to see him when he is. One of the last scenes in the book and screenplay is when Ben Hood finds the accidentally electrocuted body of Mikey Carver. Lee told Oren Moverman, "Something about that [scene] hit me really hard; it was almost like a Greek tragedy." Every relationship in the script carries the seeds of conflict.

CASTING AND FILMING *THE ICE STORM*

Fox Searchlight gave its approval for the making of *The Ice Storm* in early 1996, with a budget of $18 million, enough to attract major stars. Lee continued with his track record of casting both new stars and established ones. Katie Holmes was cast in her first movie as a girlfriend of Paul's, and Tobey Maguire was given the role of Paul. Christina Ricci, in one of her first roles, was Wendy. Elijah Wood, later to become famous in the *Lord of the Rings* trilogy, was Mikey Carver. Established stars Sigourney Weaver (playing Janey Carver), Kevin Kline (Ben Hood), and Joan Allen (Elena Hood) were cast and gave some of the most powerful performances of their careers. It was a remarkable group of actors, a sign of Lee's growing status in Hollywood.

Lee wanted the authenticity of filming in New Canaan instead of on a set. In April 1996, the cast and crew arrived, including book author Rick Moody, who later told Schamus what an incredible experience it was to see his fictional characters

Ang Lee spoke with actress Sigourney Weaver on the set of his 1997 film *The Ice Storm*, which was set in suburban Connecticut in 1973. In an interview, Weaver said, "Ang radiates kindness and compassion."

come to life. The shoot was not easy: Summer had come early, so the scenes depicting late November and an ice storm had to be filmed in 90-degree heat (32 degrees Celsius). Residents of New Canaan started to worry that the film would be unflattering, and some became hostile to the shooting.

But Lee inspired his actors, as usual. Sigourney Weaver told Laura Winters, "Ang radiates kindness and compassion. . . . I told him during the second week that I didn't think I would want to work with anyone else ever again." But Joan Allen also told Richard Mowe that Lee is "very blunt and very specific and he won't settle for less than what he wants." He had Allen, Kline, and Maguire practice walking across a room together. He felt that family members have subtle connections to one another, and having the actors walk in a similar way would help establish that they were a family. Body language is always very important to Lee.

The postproduction experience was his most difficult yet. He had shot the movie with many light-hearted moments, but with the death of the boy at the end, those moments seemed out of place, and many were replaced with a sense of foreboding about the ice storm itself as a natural disaster with devastating effects. He had to weave in elements of a horror story and a natural disaster into elements of a family drama. He was mixing genres, or "vibes" (as Lee calls them), something that he was becoming known for as a director.

On September 27, 1997, *The Ice Storm* was released. *New York Times* reporter Evelyn Nieves wrote that, in New Canaan and in Manhattan, "it's as if people had seen two different films." In a sense, they had; the mixing of vibes, of genres, can make a movie harder to market. The New Canaanites tended to dismiss the portrayal of their town, while Manhattanites buzzed about life in the suburbs. The movie was a disappointment at the box office, taking in only $8 million, the first financial loss for a Lee movie (although DVD and video sales have since made it profitable).

MOVING ON UP TO LARCHMONT

Just before *The Ice Storm* was released, Lee was finally talked into buying a home of his own. He had rented the 800-square-foot apartment in White Plains since 1986, and Schamus teased him, "Come on, man, it's time [to buy a house.]"

Lee told journalist Jennifer Frey: "We drove the kids nuts looking for houses every weekend." Jane Lin still needed to be close to her job in Valhalla, so they looked in the surrounding area. When she and Lee asked to see a small cottage on muddy marshland in Larchmont, New York, their broker assumed they would reject it. Instead, they immediately fell in love with it, especially the marsh setting. They moved in and soon started to take the train into the city, the same train that the characters in *The Ice Storm* took. They have lived in the same house in Larchmont ever since.

Soon after they moved, Lee got a phone call one day from his wife saying that a baby chick she had brought home from work had escaped into the marsh and died. The boys were crying into the phone. To comfort them, Lin bought some other chicks. Soon, "Jane and the kids were raising chickens." Frey reports that this led to a dispute with his neighbors, forcing Lee to move a chicken coop to the back of his property. It is still there.

TAKING ON MORE AMERICAN TURMOIL: *RIDE WITH THE DEVIL*

Lee was ready for more challenges and genres. He told interviewer David Schwartz, "I wanted to make a war movie." He chose a Civil War movie that became *Ride with the Devil*. The story and script fascinated Lee. Two young friends, Jake Roedel and Jack Bull Chiles, are caught up in the American Civil War when they join a band of guerrillas in Missouri known as "bushwhackers." They fight for the Confederate cause but are really only loyal to each other, their families, and Missouri itself. They fight small battles that resemble modern gang fights more than battles between armies, a realistic portrayal of the bushwhackers in Kansas and Missouri during the Civil War.

Universal Pictures gave Lee a large $38 million budget, and as usual Lee and his producers hired a fascinating cast. Tobey Maguire and Skeet Ulrich were the leads, acting with pop singer Jewel and relatively unknown actors Jonathan Rhys Meyers, Mark Ruffalo, James Caviezel, and Simon Baker.

Almost all of them have gone on to major careers in film and television.

As usual, the cast was also expected to prepare in depth. Lee asked that they read huge folders on the American history of the period. When journalist Liese Spencer suggested that Lee liked to put education into the business of film, he agreed. But he went on to say that he believed education was needed to see both sides of a story. Growing up in Taiwan, he had only heard the anti-Communist story. There was another side, just as the American Civil War had two sides. Lee believes that in

The pop singer Jewel and actor Skeet Ulrich appear in a scene from Ang Lee's Civil War-era film *Ride with the Devil*. The 1999 movie had trouble finding an audience. With his last two films failing to make back their investments, Lee was no longer in demand in Hollywood.

any conflict there is seldom pure right or pure wrong. He felt his art should increase sympathy for both sides.

The filming was done on location in western Missouri, and Lee enjoyed the outdoors life of the shoot during all four seasons—he would later say that some of the best times of his life were during the shooting of that movie. The actors and the director bonded during what seemed like an extended camping trip in some of America's most beautiful country, with rolling hills and tall-grass prairies. Lee took the actors paintball shooting and put them in a "boot camp" with weapons training and snacks consisting of food common at the time of the Civil War, including salt pork bacon. Lee told Spencer how filming *Ride with the Devil* was such a different experience:

> It feels a lot more macho, both as a person and as a filmmaker. You have a big production to take care of. You have action and safety to worry about. All I did before was kitchens and bedrooms. I used to shoot my films in a quarter of a room. Now I'm making movies where the stage is a whole town and you have to burn it down.

The movie *Ride with the Devil* was released on November 24, 1999. It never found an audience, partly because the studio went through four major personnel changes and the marketing of the film suffered, and partly because the story was complicated, with few black-and-white messages or heroes. Also, the movie lasted almost two-and-a-half hours, with long stretches between action scenes, and it used language true to the period—long flowing sentences with some words barely familiar to today's audiences. It did have some fans—singer Bruce Springsteen called it his favorite film of the year—but it made less than $1 million and still has not turned a profit.

Lee's career now had its first failures. His last two movies had not made back their investments. In Hollywood terms, he was no longer "hot." Suddenly, the flow of scripts slowed to a trickle. He needed a new start, so he went back to the culture he knew best. He journeyed to China to make one of the most famous movies of all time.

6

The Best of Times, the Worst of Times, 2000–2004

Even before he made *Pushing Hands,* Ang Lee had said there was one movie he always wanted to make. Growing up, he was fascinated by martial-arts movies, and he knew the genre so well it was second nature. As a director, he always wanted to take a genre he knew well and mix it with another. He now knew how to do romantic drama about the tensions between and within people. He had the idea to combine martial arts with serious romantic drama. Lee told journalist Richard Mowe, "The idea of making a martial-arts film with great drama and visual style is a longtime dream. Somehow, inevitably, I was going this way."

Lee had grown up with a series of adventure books about China hundreds of years ago. The books were part of *wuxia* (translated as "martial-arts chivalry") literature dating to the third or fourth century, about brave warriors with extraordinary fighting skills and abilities. These warriors believed in personal freedom and serving the poor and less fortunate—they were often accomplished swordsmen enforcing a code of chivalry. Well

WUXIA AND KUNG FU MOVIES

Critics and fans have many ways of categorizing Chinese martial-arts films. Some divide them up according to where they were filmed: Hong Kong, Taiwan, or Mainland China. Others describe them by whether they feature Wudang or Shaolin martial-arts techniques: Wudang emphasizes defense and "soft" techniques, Shaolin offense and "hard" techniques—explosive fists and kicks.

One of the most common ways is to distinguish between "wuxia" and "kung fu" movies. In wuxia films, including *Crouching Tiger, Hidden Dragon,* people most often use swords and spears as their featured weapons, while in kung fu movies, the characters traditionally use only their fists and feet. Wuxia fighters can also use a staff, sewing needles, ink brushes, or anything that can be thrown with accuracy. The wuxia tradition often features a strong woman warrior and a plot line including some romance. The kung fu movie is usually more about brotherhood and man-to-man relationships. Wuxia films usually have an element of the supernatural and superhuman, with actors flying or performing incredible acrobatic feats (aided by ultra-thin wires removed in postproduction). Actors glide on walls or skim on treetops, as in *Crouching Tiger, Hidden Dragon.*

Bruce Lee launched a worldwide kung fu movie and television craze in the early 1970s. Bruce Lee legends are everywhere, including his two-finger pushups and his one-inch punch—legend has it that he could knock down someone by starting his punch one inch from the opponent, without shifting his weight. His death in 1973, three weeks before the release of his last movie, *Enter the Dragon,* is still a mystery at many levels.

Of course, "wuxia" and "kung fu" have now almost merged, so the distinction is mostly historical. Jackie Chan and Jet Li (a five-time national Chinese martial-arts champion) have blurred this distinction between wuxia and kung fu by combining elements of crime drama, comedy, Chinese gangs (triads), guns, knives, and car chases into faster-paced martial-arts dramas.

before the British and European tales of knights serving their kings and heroically saving young maidens, the *wuxia* warriors walked the earth and dispensed justice outside the law. Women warriors were often a part of the *wuxia* tradition—strong, chivalric, and every bit as effective as fighters as male warriors.

Soon, a script was developed for Lee by his best friend James Schamus and two Chinese writers. It was called *Crouching Tiger, Hidden Dragon*, and it outlined two romances. One was between an older martial-arts master, Li Mu Bai, and an experienced and skilled woman warrior, Yu Shu Lien. The other involved two young lovers, Jen and Lo. Jen is the daughter of an aristocrat who is secretly training to be a master warrior, and Lo is a bandit. A fifth main character is Jade Fox, the closest thing to a villain, someone who has murdered Mu Bai's master. The plot winds around the theft and return of a magical jade sword named "Green Destiny." Like "Excalibur" of King Arthur fame, it has powers that make its owner almost invincible.

MAKING *CROUCHING TIGER, HIDDEN DRAGON*

Lee had to go to several sources to obtain funding for the project, from China, Taiwan, Hong Kong, and three American companies—Columbia, Sony Classics, and Good Machine. He was given a budget of $15 million, much less than his last two films, and he had to agree not to take a salary for himself. He was no longer "golden" in Hollywood terms. But he did have his reputation. Lee was known for working closely with actors and crew members and demanding their best performances, so the best performers and crew members gravitated to him.

Two of the world's most famous and accomplished actors at the time were Chow Yun-Fat (born and working mostly in Hong Kong), who agreed to be Li Mu Bai, and Michelle Yeoh (born in Malaysia and also based in Hong Kong), who was signed to be Yu Shu Lien. New actor Zhang Ziyi was given the part of Jen.

Zhang Ziyi *(left)* and Chow Yun-Fat soar through the trees during a scene from *Crouching Tiger, Hidden Dragon.* A *wuxia* film like *Crouching Tiger* often had an element of the supernatural or superhuman in it. With *Crouching Tiger*, Ang Lee sought to mix genres by making a martial-arts film that had serious romantic drama.

One of the most important members of the film crew was Yuen Wo-Ping, who had recently choreographed fight scenes in the classic movie *The Matrix.* He had worked with Jackie Chan and Jet Li, and this film gave him another chance to prove that he was the best martial-arts choreographer in film. After Lee saw *The Matrix,* he knew it was time to do a martial-arts movie in a big way.

The filming was based in Beijing, China. Lee had never visited Mainland China before but had imagined it ever since he was a small child. He told *New York Times* reporter Erik Eckholm, "This is going back to my cultural roots as well as my fantasy." The movie was mostly shot on location in many hard-to-reach places, including the Gobi Desert and the Taklamakan Plateau north of Tibet. The cast and crew got lost the first night of shooting in the Gobi and were not found until 7 A.M. the following day. They often stayed in low-budget hotels to save money. They hiked for miles to get to their shooting locations. Shooting was not easy—it rained for days in the Gobi Desert (a very dry place normally), and the stunts performed by the actors were difficult. Yeoh tore knee ligaments during the first week, and shooting had to be rearranged while she rehabilitated for five weeks. The film seemed cursed.

Eckholm wrote that, when he visited the filming at a Beijing studio in December 1999, the set was freezing and Lee could be seen in a heavy blue parka trying to get a fight sequence just right. Zhang's character had to fight off an attacker, ripping his sleeve. After dozens of takes, the actors were exhausted and Lee was still trying to get exactly the look he wanted. Fight after fight, scene after scene, Lee was a perfectionist. Eckholm quoted Lee as saying, "This is the toughest shoot I've ever had. It's hard to put martial arts and drama together."

REAPING THE REWARDS OF A GREAT MOVIE

All the suffering and effort paid off. Maximum effort brought maximum results. The movie was released in the United States on December 22, 2000, and critics loved it. *Rolling Stone* movie critic Peter Travers wrote, "Here is the kind of filmmaking magic that we've been missing for ages." Some felt that it blended the best of movies like *The Matrix* with love stories like *Titanic*. Writer Jay Carr said the movie "teaches motion pictures a few new things about motion. Watching it is a nonstop high." The movie went on to make more than $128 million in North America and $213 million worldwide. It is still the most successful foreign-language movie to be shown in North America. It was also a hit in the awards sweepstakes, getting four Oscars (including one for "Best Foreign-Language Film"), two Golden

Globe awards (including one for "Best Director"), and dozens of other tributes.

For the very first time in his life, Ang Lee was world famous. But Jane Lin told *New York Times* reporter Kate Stone Lombardi, "Fame is not going to change him." The fame was a reward for all the nights Lee could not be home with his family. Later in his life, he would say it was a sacrifice he felt he had to make.

When Lee went on stage to receive his Golden Globe award for "Best Director," one of his assistants called Lin and held his phone to his television so she could hear Lee's acceptance speech. Lee and Lin did not own a television, and their

Crouching Tiger, Hidden Dragon won four Academy Awards, including one for "Best Foreign-Language Film." Celebrating the victory were *(from left)* actress Michelle Yeoh; actor Chow Yun-Fat's wife, Jasmine; Chow Yun-Fat; and Ang Lee. The film is the most successful foreign-language film in North America.

son Haan was studying for his advanced-placement American history test the next day. Lin was worried that all the calls coming in would disturb his studies. She told Lombardi, "We were a little bothered that night. People were calling from different time zones and waking us, and I was thinking, 'If he [Haan] fails his test, we know who to blame.'" Fame was not going to change Lin either.

Among his many honors for *Crouching Tiger, Hidden Dragon,* Lee received an honorary doctorate from New York University in May 2001. He was thrilled, as was his father. Lee had disappointed his father with his academic failures so many years ago, but he now had a doctorate. He was not only famous but was now successful in the eyes of the one person who still doubted his career. His father would never doubt him again.

TAKING ON A SUPER ANTIHERO

With the success of *Crouching Tiger, Hidden Dragon,* Lee was "hot" again. The scripts and ideas for scripts came at him from every direction. Lee, as always, wanted to do something different, and the next challenge he would set for himself was to do a big-budget Hollywood blockbuster. In some ways, it represented the greatest test for a director.

Hollywood insiders at the time knew that three kinds of movies get made with big budgets: films with Leonardo DiCaprio, successful sequels, and comic-book hero movies. No one knows if Lee or Schamus approached DiCaprio, but they did briefly consider doing a sequel, *Terminator 3.* They decided that film would not give them enough freedom. Instead, they turned their attention to comic books.

Marvel Comics writers Stan Lee and Jack Kirby created three superheroes/sets of heroes in less than one year (November 1961 to August 1962): the Fantastic Four, the Hulk, and Spider-Man. These superheroes had superpowers but personal problems as well, and a generation of new comic-book readers grew up with them.

Lee toyed with the idea of doing a "Fantastic Four" film, but a project was already in development. Schamus knew that a proposal for "The Hulk" had been around Universal Studios for years but had not been made. He sent Lee a project description and said that it was a good subject for him—essentially a story of repressed emotions that get let out in a big way. The Hulk was different from other Marvel Comics superheroes and was really not a superhero at all. He was more like King Kong—a force to be feared but understood and pitied as well. Some called him an antihero, because he was not fighting for truth and justice as other superheroes were, but instead was destructive and out of control.

. Lee loved comic books growing up but had not read *The Hulk*. He remembered the character from the television series in the 1970s, starring Bill Bixby as Bruce Banner and Lou Ferrigno as the Hulk. He felt a connection to the subject, as cited by *Newsweek's* Devin Gordon:

> To Lee, all his movies—including *Hulk*—are about the same thing: emotional repression. "It clicked right away," he [Lee] says. "I call Hulk my new Green Destiny [the sword in *Crouching Tiger*]. Both films are about the real you that you try to cover up with your culture and your character. It's the darker side, the anger."

Schamus revised a previously written script for *The Hulk*. In the new script, Bruce Banner has been infected with mutant DNA because of genetic experiments done by his father, David Banner, an irresponsible scientist who accidentally killed his wife (Bruce's mother) and was sent to a mental hospital. The 4-year-old Bruce was adopted, not knowing his father was still alive. Bruce gradually discovers his own mutant DNA, and after an accident in a lab, his raging Hulk-self is activated. Bruce's ex-girlfriend and co-researcher Betty Ross tries to help him understand what is happening and protect him from the military people interested in his research. When his father reappears to learn more about his son's work, their conflicts escalate until they battle it out on an epic scale near the movie's end.

MAKING *THE HULK*

Universal gave Lee and Schamus $150 million to film a true Hollywood blockbuster, by far the biggest budget Lee had ever received. Not even the sky was the limit. Lee was persuaded that, unlike the television series, the Hulk needed to be very big and very bad. An actor simply could not be made to represent something up to 15 feet (4.5 meters) high. Both animatronics (robots made to look like people or animals) and computer-generated imagery (CGI) had become commonplace by 2000, and Lee decided to learn about them.

Producer Larry Franco showed him exactly how *Jurassic Park 3* had been done, shot by shot, and they visited several animatronics companies. Lee became convinced that CGI and not animatronics was what he wanted to use to make the Hulk. George Lucas's company, Industrial Light and Magic (ILM), was contracted to do much of the computer rendering of the Hulk.

Australian actor Eric Bana was signed on to be Bruce Banner, and Jennifer Connelly was Betty Ross. Lee persuaded Nick Nolte to be David Banner. Lee told interviewer Paul Fischer that his first meeting with Nolte was unforgettable:

> I went to his house in Hollywood and it was the most gothic experience I ever had. It was this weird collection of stuff from around the world. And I was sitting by the fireplace and after five minutes he said, "You must come up and see my blood." And I went upstairs and there was a lab with hundreds of bottles of something

Ang Lee worked in postproduction for six months on the computer-generated imagery to create the monster in *The Hulk*. In this scene, the military pursues the Hulk through the streets of San Francisco. Unfortunately, many moviegoers thought that the Hulk did not look realistic.

and there's an electronic monitor. So he pricks his own finger and watches on this monitor his own [blood] cells . . . and I said something like you can make it more colorful and he was impressed.

Filming began on March 18, 2002, in Arizona, moved to San Francisco on April 19, and then to Utah, deserts in California, and finally to a stage set in Los Angeles in July. Bana told reporters that the film sets were very serious, with little of the on-set playfulness that some movies have. A Lee filming was usually a serious affair, but the blockbuster budget made it even more so. The most extensive part of the filming was at Industrial Light and Magic. Lee literally had to live at ILM for six months and put on a virtual-reality suit to get the facial expressions and body language he wanted for the Hulk. Lee was seen going from workstation to workstation asking for a change in a Hulk eyelash or the way Hulk wrinkled his brow. ILM logged more than 2 million hours of computer time to make parts of *The Hulk* and did not finish until May 2003, a month before the movie was released. Dennis Muren, ILM's director of special effects at the time, told *Newsweek*'s Devin Gordon that he had worked with all the great directors—Lucas, Steven Spielberg, James Cameron, even Stanley Kubrick. Muren said Lee was more demanding and passionate than any of them, with the possible exception of Kubrick.

The postproduction editing of *The Hulk* included a groundbreaking use of different panels on the movie screen at the same time, just as a comic book has different panels on a page. Lee told film critic Elvis Mitchell:

> I had to find my way of translating the excitement you get when you're reading comic books to the screen. Not just lining up things with montage, but choreographing multi-images in the same space—which is something I'd always thought about doing, but this was the perfect excuse to try it out. I think the time is right for that kind of film language, because it's the way media is going.

A SUMMER MOVIE MORE FIZZLING THAN SIZZLING

The movie was released on June 20, 2003, as a summer blockbuster. Its marketing pointed to a contradiction in the movie itself. The theme tag line "The inner beast will be released" alternated with "Unleash the hero within." So, anger is considered both heroic and destructive, and audiences were not quite sure what they were getting—a hero or an antihero or both. Also, 150 items with a *Hulk* logo were developed, leading Lee to joke that Universal was marketing everything that was green.

Many fans were disappointed. Some felt that the Hulk was puffy and fake-looking. His three-mile (4.8-kilometer) leaps and 300-mile-per-hour (483-kilometer-per-hour) speed were impressive but hard to relate to. Others felt that the multi-paneled screens did not add anything to the experience. The movie became bogged down in family dramas, some said.

Lee was always exhausted at the end of a movie, but after making *The Hulk* for almost three years and seeing that it was not an immediate hit, he considered leaving directing for good. His father was the one who persuaded him to not give up his career. Lee told *New York Times* reporter Jennifer Frey that his father said, "You have to go on, you can't quit." During the time of his greatest professional failure, Lee drew strength and support from his father. It was one of the last times he would hear from his father.

So, Lee remained a director. He plunged back into moviemaking. He was soon sent a script for a small movie that had no CGI, no big budget, and no blockbuster expectations. The script was named *Brokeback Mountain*. He told Frey that he thought the film "wouldn't get much attention." It was to become one of the world's most influential and controversial films.

7

To the Top of the Mountain and Beyond, 2005–2009

Annie Proulx is a Pulitzer Prize-winning author whose story "Brokeback Mountain" appeared in *The New Yorker* magazine on October 13, 1997. The story is about two ranch hands, Ennis Del Mar and Jack Twist, who are hired to herd sheep on a remote mountain in 1963. The story is set in the Big Horn Mountains of Wyoming. Brokeback Mountain is a fictional place but is probably based on a combination of Mount Lougheed and Moose Mountain, which combine to make a curved ridge, or "brokeback," named after a mule or horse with a swayed back.

Ennis and Jack are 19 when they meet, without friends and poor. The story describes them as "a pair of deuces going nowhere." They are actually very different people but become friends as they work together, cook, and talk during their period of isolation on the mountain. One night, after drinking whiskey for hours, they turn to each other for physical intimacy and then develop a sexual relationship. Their relationship becomes a kind of extreme friendship, but one that needs to be covered up. When their summer ends, they separate. Each gets married and has children, but their bond is so strong that they need to see each other on rare camping trips. Jack wants to buy a ranch together, but Ennis fears they will be killed if anyone finds out about their relationship.

Proulx told *Newsweek* writer Sean Smith, "This is a deep, permanent human condition, this need to be loved and to love. While I was working on this story, I was occasionally close to tears. I felt guilty their lives were so difficult, yet there was nothing I could do about it."

Annie Proulx's short story "Brokeback Mountain" was published in *The New Yorker* in 1997. Proulx did not begin to publish her fiction until she was in her 50s. She won the National Book Award and Pulitzer Prize for her novel *The Shipping News*.

MAKING THE UNMAKABLE MOVIE

Writers Larry McMurtry and Diana Ossana wrote a script based on the short story, but no studio wanted to make the movie. When a director was interested, no actors could be found who were willing to take the risk of having their careers ruined with a "gay" role. So, the script was shelved for years. It became known as the best script for a movie never to be made.

One day, a movie producer named William Pohlad (son of billionaire banker and former Minnesota Twins owner Carl Pohlad) read the *Brokeback* script on a plane and told his wife that he finally found a movie he wanted to finance.

ANNIE PROULX

The author of the short story "Brokeback Mountain" is Edna Annie Proulx (pronounced "prew"). She was born in Norwich, Connecticut, in 1935, but her family moved all around New England when she was a child. Since she lived mostly in books, the moves did not bother her too much.

Later, she lived for more than 30 years in Vermont and moved to Wyoming in 1994, where she has lived since. She often spends summers in northern Newfoundland, Canada. She is a student of wild and lonely places and the people who live in them.

She and Ang Lee have much in common. Like Lee, she was a late bloomer—she did not start publishing her fictional stories until she was in her 50s. She won the National Book Award and the Pulitzer Prize for her second book, *The Shipping News*, which was published in 1993. She too is intense and single-minded in her work habits, and her attention to detail is legendary. She may research knife-making for days to write only one sentence about it. She also gets completely absorbed in her work and her

His entertainment company, River Road, made a deal with Schamus, who had been recruited to be co-president of Focus Features, a production company owned by Universal Studios. Around the same time, Lee was looking for his next project. With Schamus's help, he found it. Soon, casting and filming began for the movie nobody ever thought could be made.

When Jake Gyllenhaal was cast as Jack Twist and Heath Ledger as Ennis Del Mar, some in Hollywood felt sorry for the two young actors. One typical producer told *Newsweek*'s Sean Smith that their careers might be over, and teenage girls would be alienated from them. Ledger told Smith:

characters. Proulx has been known to write for 18 hours at a time when she is seized by a plot twist or a character.

Like Lee, she believes in and writes about change. She told *Boston Globe* reporter Patti Dotten, "What interests me is social change—the melting away of older ways of living and thinking." She also, like Lee, believes in forces both hidden and open: "I believe in natural forces. And humans are part of those natural forces." In one of her stories, an ice storm changes the characters forever.

When Proulx saw the movie *Brokeback Mountain,* she was delighted. She noted to *Village Voice* writer Jessica Winter that the movie was "marvelous, huge. I'm not sure I can put into words the sensation of seeing something you've written years ago rear up in monstrous size before you."

Proulx was called to serve on a jury in the case of the murder of 21-year-old student Matthew Shepard in Laramie, Wyoming, some 30 miles (48 kilometers) from her home. Shepard was gay, and beaten and left to die tied to a fence post by two men on October 6, 1998, almost a year after "Brokeback Mountain" was published. Proulx was not selected for the jury.

I never thought twice about it. . . . I think if you make decisions based on society's opinions, you're going to make boring choices. What terrified me was self-doubt. I knew that, if I was going to do justice to this character, to this story and this form of love, I was really going to have to mature as an actor, and as a person.

Gyllenhaal felt the same way, thinking the script was so well done that he had to be in the movie.

The filming ran through the summer of 2004, almost entirely in the Canadian Rockies. As with the filming of *Ride with the Devil*, Lee enjoyed being outdoors and camping under a star-filled sky. His family came to visit him twice. He told several journalists that he was very relaxed during the shoot. After the ordeal of making *The Hulk*, this was simple and easy, letting the film unfold.

When entertainment journalists asked Schamus how Focus Features and Universal would market the film when many young men watching the trailer for the movie were laughing and snickering, Schamus replied, "If you have a problem with the subject matter, that's your problem, not mine. It would be great if you got over your problem, but I'm not sitting here trying to help you with it." Schamus also knew the target audience was not gay men, but women.

THE WORLD'S RESPONSE TO *BROKEBACK MOUNTAIN*

Brokeback Mountain was released in New York, Los Angeles, and San Francisco on December 9, 2005, and then put into wider release over the next few weeks, letting word of mouth and controversy build. The old saying that all publicity is good

Ang Lee works with Heath Ledger *(center)* and Jake Gyllenhaal on the set of *Brokeback Mountain*. Much of the filming took place in the Rocky Mountains in Canada. In interviews, Lee said he was very relaxed during the shoot.

publicity seemed to be coming true. Soon audiences were flocking to see the film, often with women bringing men.

Most critics loved the film. It won four Golden Globe awards (including "Best Drama" and "Best Director") on January 16, 2006, helping increase its box-office draw even more. On March 5, Lee was named "Best Director" at the Academy Awards, and the film picked up Oscars for the musical score and McMurtry and Ossana's screenplay. After the Oscars, the commercial success of the movie rose—the movie has now made roughly $178 million on an investment of $14 million.

The firestorm of controversy the film set off had many parts. Some felt that the two men were bisexual, not gay, and that bisexuality was really the focus of the film. Others felt that Ennis was heterosexual in his nature and homosexual only toward Jack. Ledger himself told *Time* magazine, "I don't think Ennis could be labeled as gay. Without Jack Twist, I don't know that he ever would have come out. . . . I think the whole point was that it was two souls that fell in love with each other." Critic Eric Marcus is quoted as saying that "talk of Ennis and Jack being anything but gay [is] box office-induced political correctness intended to steer straight audiences to the film." Some felt that any and all labels were demeaning in simplifying complex sexual-identity issues. Others said that the whole point of the movie was not their being gay, but their being told to hide who they were. They needed to break free from society's expectations.

The movie has become part of our cultural landscape. In late 2008, the New York City Opera commissioned an opera based on the story and the movie, to be performed in 2013. The film's last scene shows Ennis embracing Jack's shirt. That shirt sold on eBay for more than $100,000.

ANOTHER FILM SET IN CHINA

Lee's fame after winning his "Best Director" award spread throughout the world. He was now very much in demand again. In October 2006, the organizing committee for the 2008 Beijing Olympics persuaded him to become a consultant for the opening and closing ceremonies. They were spectacular. *Time* listed him as one of the 100 "People Who Shape Our World" in 2006.

He was ready for his next world-shaping movie, and he decided to look for material in another classic short story, not a comic book or a novel, for another "small movie." He found inspiration in Chinese writer Eileen Chang's "Lust, Caution," published in 1979. The story was a portrayal of Japanese forces occupying China during World War II. It focused on a powerful

Chinese official named Mr. Yee, who is helping the Japanese in Shanghai in 1942, and a young woman, Wong Chia Chi, who is part of a resistance group of Chinese university students determined to assassinate Mr. Yee. Wong Chia Chi must become Mr. Yee's lover to get close to him, but when the time comes to assassinate him, she cannot. She has fallen in love with her oppressor, or at least bonded with him in a way she did not expect. He, on the other hand, has her killed when he finds out about the plot against him. Like many Lee movies, this one was

Ang Lee returned to China for the setting of his 2007 film, *Lust, Caution*. Here, he appears with actress Tang Wei and actor Wang Lee-Hom before the premiere of the film in Shanghai. The movie did quite well in China but had a much smaller audience in the United States, mostly because it was given an NC-17 rating.

about a hidden relationship, with hidden emotions expressing themselves powerfully.

Lee told *New York Times* columnist Dennis Lim that, when he read the story, he could not stop thinking about it, which is usually a signal that it has awakened something deeper in him and that an audience might feel the same way. Lee told Lim, "There's a point where I feel this is my story. It becomes a mission."

As with many of his movies, Lee used a cast of new actors blended with experienced ones. Mr. Yee was played by Tony Leung, a famous Chinese actor with many starring roles to his credit. Wong Chia Chi was played by a newcomer, Tang Wei. The cast also included famous actress Joan Chen as Mrs. Yee. The filming was difficult because the movie contained explicit sex scenes.

The movie was released in Taiwan first, on September 24, 2007, and in the United States four days later, earning an NC-17 rating (no one 17 or under is admitted). That rating guarantees a small audience in America—audiences often shun films with an NC-17 rating, and some theater owners refuse to show them. *Lust, Caution* has not been seen by many Americans but has done well in China.

LIFE CONTINUES

New York Times reporter Jennifer Frey interviewed Lee in depth in November 2007 and found that his lifestyle is the same one he has had for years. He rarely uses a computer or a cell phone. In the backyard of his Larchmont house, he still has a chicken coop, not a swimming pool. Lee told Frey, "I don't lead a Hollywood lifestyle. In Taiwan, I'd be like Michael Jordan walking down the street. Here I can live a normal life and still make movies in the city." He's still shy.

Haan graduated from Mamaroneck High School in 2002 and went on to Brown University. Mason was a senior at

Mamaroneck High when Frey interviewed Lee, accomplished in playing the cello and performing in the school's theater group. Jane Lin volunteers regularly backstage with the theater group, and once when she was sick, Lee replaced her. Barbara Whitman, another involved parent, told Frey, "He was wonderful. He's very unassuming. You'd never know who he was, unless you knew." Lee spoke at length about his life: "I feel bad," he said. "I never saw Haan in a fencing competition. I missed all his games. I missed most of his teenage years." But he said Lin and his sons backed his ambitions. "It's an us thing," he said. "I cannot do it alone. I need the support of them. We have no regrets. I missed some of the family life, but those are good movies. They're worth the effort." Unlike many artists, Lee is not anxious about the value of his work. His sacrifice is one that filmgoers are grateful for.

Lee never stays idle for long. As of April 2009, he was in postproduction for *Taking Woodstock*, a film about the famous music festival in upstate New York in August 1969. It stars comedian Demetri Martin as Elliot Tiber, one of the planners of the legendary event. It is advertised as a comedy, but knowing the director it will be a blend of genres and will explore hot-button themes.

THE ANG LEE LEGACY

Ang Lee has left a lasting legacy through his films. His characters are often unable to voice their feelings and their desires, so he uses silence and gestures to show and not tell what they are feeling. He exposes on film our unresolved feelings and desires and how they can hurt us and make us prisoners if we don't resolve them.

He has used his imagination to make his dreams and fantasies become real in art, bringing deep and dark impulses into the flickering light of cinema to help us see what we are

(continues on page 104)

REVOLUTION

Ang Lee was a teenager during the famously rebellious 1960s, a time that widened the gap between generations in almost every part of the world. Lee was not very rebellious outwardly, but he did take a very different path in life from the one his parents wanted for him.

Lee is a student of the 1960s. His next movie is based on the memoir *Taking Woodstock* by Elliot Tiber, a New York City interior designer whose parents owned the only music festival permit in the small town of Bethel, New York. Tiber offers the permit to the organizers of the Woodstock Music Festival, setting the stage for a generation-defining event in August 1969.

The 1960s strengthened the idea of a generation gap, both for Americans and Asian Americans, and that gap became defined as partly political. The civil-rights movement that began in the 1950s and centered on African Americans spread to other ethnic groups in the 1960s. Students all over the world began to speak out against the conservative politics of their parents, especially in the United States.

For example, some Asian-American students in the San Francisco area joined a group called the Third World Liberation Front. The group asked for a political alliance among Asian, African, Latin, and Native Americans. It demanded that ethnic studies departments be formed at various universities and called for a student strike if their demands were not met. Some Asians called for solidarity among their own—"ABCs" (American-born Chinese) had to share political goals with "FOBs" (Fresh off the Boat). The Third World Liberation Front and other student groups led the 1968 student strike at San Francisco State University, which remains one of the longest campus shutdowns in history. The generations clashed over the strike, as most parents of activists felt that, because education was so important, a college should never be shut down, however worthy the goal.

Political activism, though, had its limits. Author Gish Jen describes the life of a young Chinese woman living in the New York suburbs in the 1960s in her novel *Mona in the Promised Land*. Mona and her friends discuss bringing a political revolution to the United States but also worry about their SAT scores and getting into college. Mona is very impatient with her immigrant parents, and shares her thoughts about them:

> "You know, the Chinese revolution was a long time ago; you can get over it now. Okay, so you had to hide in the garden and listen to bombs fall out of the sky, also you lost everything you had. And it's true you don't even know what happened to your sisters and brothers and parents. . . . But didn't you make it? Aren't you here in America, watching the sale ads. . . . You know what you are now?" she wants to say. "Now you're smart shoppers." . . . But in another way she understands it's like asking the Jews to get over the Holocaust, or like asking the blacks to get over slavery.

Jen's novel points out that a gap developed between parents and children during the 1960s specifically about the differences between living through the Chinese Civil War, which the parents had, and being born after it. The world did not seem to be the same place to the two generations. Some Taiwanese parents were locked in the past, focused on what they had lost. Their children, growing up in the 1960s, had a much different view. They did not know China firsthand, and many did not want to go there. Both Taiwan and China seemed repressive to them. The social, political, and sexual freedom promised by the United States in the 1960s was what called to them, and the call was heard loudest around the rolling farmlands of Woodstock.

(continued from page 101)

made of. As he said to critic Rick Lyman, he wants "to reach that juicy part that is very vulnerable and that you can only reach when you are in the dark, in a movie theater, and you are with people."

Like all great artists, he asks us to increase our sympathy for others. He demonstrates that many types of people exist in the world and that we enlarge ourselves when we get to know about them. He wants his audience to respect other cultures. If we all have an instinct to be part of a community, then Ang Lee's community is the world itself. He often saw himself as an outsider, a foreigner, but increasingly he seems to have redefined what is inside and outside. He is both Asian and American, drawing on the strengths of both cultures.

He also shows us the sheer beauty of our world, in landscapes of England, America, and China that almost become characters themselves. His movies are filled with vivid details, textures, sights, and sounds. From mushrooms to mountains, his art draws a moving picture.

And like all great artists, he is changed by his own works of art. With *Crouching Tiger, Hidden Dragon*, he discovered the China of his dreams and turned those dreams into memories. He showed parts of America in *The Ice Storm, Ride with the Devil,* and *Brokeback Mountain* that have helped him understand his adopted and still partly foreign country.

His upbringing, experience, and training in Chinese philosophy make him a student of both emotions and our search for security. He says on the Internet Movie Database that "people want to believe in something, want to hang onto something to get security and want to trust each other. But things change. Given enough time, nothing stands still." His movies are filled with people looking for but not finding security. Change itself is the only thing that does not change.

One of the most remarkable parts of his life is that he almost did not get a chance to become a moviemaker. He had to wait and persist. Like many late bloomers, his success has depended on the ideas and support of others—Jane Lin, James Schamus, Tim Squyres, Emma Thompson, Annie Proulx, and many more. He never gave up on his dream of making films, even when he could find no one to take a chance on him for six long years.

Lee was and is fearless about what he is willing to show in his films, and what films he is willing to make. He has succeeded brilliantly but sometimes failed brilliantly as well. To make a movie, you have to care deeply about something. He cares deeply about many things. As a result, he has become the most celebrated Asian-American film director in history.

CHRONOLOGY

1954 Born on October 23 in Chaochou, Taiwan.
1963 Goes to life-changing movie, *Love Eternal,* while living in Hwalian, Taiwan.
1968 Family moves to Tainan, Taiwan; Lee goes to Tainan First Senior High School.
1972 Enters Taiwan Academy of Arts in Taipei as a theater and film student.
1975 Graduates from the academy; enters military service in Taiwan.

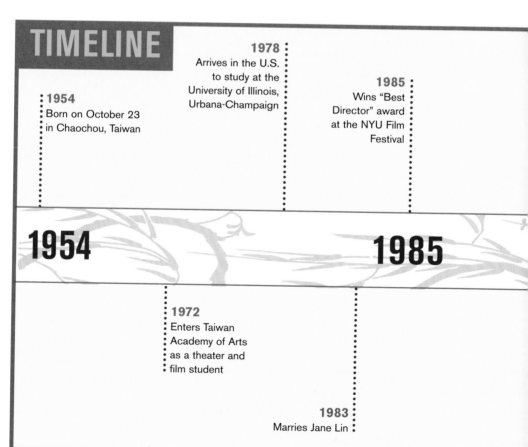

TIMELINE

1978
Arrives in the U.S. to study at the University of Illinois, Urbana-Champaign

1954
Born on October 23 in Chaochou, Taiwan

1985
Wins "Best Director" award at the NYU Film Festival

1954

1985

1972
Enters Taiwan Academy of Arts as a theater and film student

1983
Marries Jane Lin

1978 Arrives in the United States in August
to study at the University of Illinois
Urbana-Champaign; meets his future wife,
Jane Lin.

1980 Graduates from the University of Illinois
with a B.F.A. in theater/theater direction;
enters the graduate program in film production
at New York University's Tisch School of
the Arts.

1983 Marries Jane Lin in a civil ceremony in
New York City.

1984 Finishes master's thesis film *Fine Line* and
graduates with an M.F.A. in film production
in May; son Haan is born.

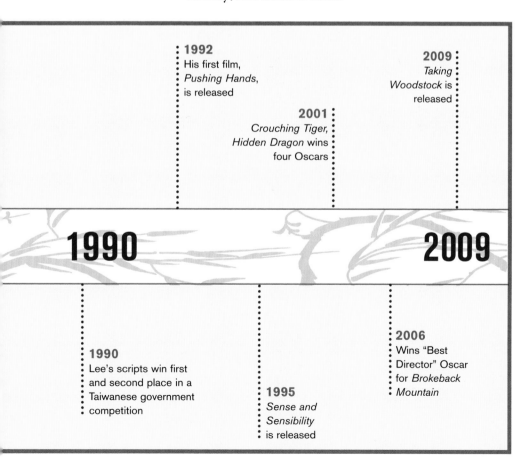

1992
His first film,
Pushing Hands,
is released

2009
*Taking
Woodstock* is
released

2001
*Crouching Tiger,
Hidden Dragon* wins
four Oscars

1990

2009

1990
Lee's scripts win first
and second place in a
Taiwanese government
competition

1995
*Sense and
Sensibility*
is released

2006
Wins "Best
Director" Oscar
for *Brokeback
Mountain*

1985 Wins "Best Director" award at NYU Film Festival and gets an agent from the William Morris Agency.

1986 Jane Lin receives her Ph.D., and the family moves to White Plains, New York.

1990 Son Mason is born; scripts by Lee win first and second place in a competition sponsored by the Taiwanese government; Central Motion Pictures Corporation of Taiwan provides financing for *Pushing Hands*.

1991 Meets James Schamus and begins to film *Pushing Hands*.

1992 *Pushing Hands* is released in Taiwan.

1993 *The Wedding Banquet* is released on August 4.

1994 *The Wedding Banquet* is nominated for a "Best Foreign-Language Film" Oscar and wins "Best Picture" at the Berlin Film Festival; *Eat Drink Man Woman* is released on August 3.

1995 *Eat Drink Man Woman* wins several international film awards. *Sense and Sensibility* is released on December 13.

1997 *The Ice Storm* is released on September 27; Lee's family buys a house in Larchmont, New York.

1999 *Ride with the Devil* is released on November 24.

2000 *Crouching Tiger, Hidden Dragon* is released on December 22.

2001 *Crouching Tiger, Hidden Dragon* wins four Oscars and two Golden Globes. Lee receives an honorary Ph.D. from New York University in May.

2003 *The Hulk* is released on June 20.

2005 *Brokeback Mountain* is released on December 9.

2006 Lee wins "Best Director" Oscar for his work on *Brokeback Mountain*.

2007 Lust, Caution is released on September 28.

2009 *Taking Woodstock* is released.

GLOSSARY

antimatter—A form of matter in which the electrical charge or other properties of each particle is the reverse of that in the usual matter of our universe.

blocking—The act of charting the movements of performers in a stage or film scene.

cinematographer—A movie photographer, especially one who is in charge of shooting a movie.

civil war—A war between opposing groups of citizens of the same country.

close-up—A movie shot taken at close range.

Communism—A political ideology that promotes the establishment of an egalitarian society based on common ownership of goods as well as control of property and the means of production.

director—A person who supervises the creative aspects of a film and instructs the actors and crew members.

distributor—The organization responsible for coordinating the distribution of a finished movie to theaters as well as the sale of DVDs and other media versions of the movie.

film editor—The person who selects and joins together shots, connecting the resulting sequences and ultimately creating a finished movie.

genre—A category of film characterized by a particular style, form, or content.

guerrilla—A member of an irregular, often politically motivated, armed force that fights regular forces.

nationalism—A sense of national consciousness exalting one nation above all others and placing primary emphasis on the promotion of its culture and interests.

pagoda—A tall tower with a distinctive steeple, usually a shrine.

pitch—To present a film idea for consideration.

postproduction—The work done on a movie after the filming has occurred. This work includes film editing.

preproduction—The arrangements made before filming begins. These activities may include scriptwriting, script editing, set construction, location scouting, and casting.

producer—A person who supervises and controls the financing, creation, and public presentation of a film.

production assistant—An often entry-level position responsible for various aspects of a film or television production. Tasks may include running errands, answering telephones, or acting as couriers. Levels of responsibility can vary greatly, depending on the project.

recession—A period of reduced economic activity.

shot—A continuous block of unedited film footage from a single point of view.

tai chi—An ancient Chinese discipline of meditative movements practiced as a system of exercises.

take—A single continuous recorded performance of a scene. Directors typically order more takes until they are satisfied that all their requirements for the scene, artistic and technical, have been met.

trailer—An advertisement for a movie that contains scenes from the film.

BIBLIOGRAPHY

Bloom, Dan. "Ang Lee's Current Project Has a Backstory of Pure Serendipity." *Taipei Times*, October 11, 2008.

Carr, Jay. "High Flying 'Tiger' Ang Lee's Latest Film Trips the Martial Arts Fantastic." *The Boston Globe*, December 22, 2000.

Chang, Iris. *The Chinese in America: A Narrative History*. New York: Penguin Books, 2003.

Dilley, Whitney Crothers. *The Cinema of Ang Lee: The Other Side of the Screen*. London: Wallflower Press, 2007.

Eckholm, Erik. "A Filmmaker Reroutes the Flow of History." *The New York Times*, December 16, 1999.

Farhi, Paul. "You Know You've Arrived . . ." *The Washington Post*, March 5, 2006.

Fischer, Paul. "Ang Lee Tackles the Hulk." *Film Monthly*, June 14, 2003.

Frey, Jennifer. "A Chicken Coop, but No Tigers." *The New York Times*, November 25, 2007.

Gladwell, Malcolm. *Outliers: The Story of Success*. New York: Little, Brown, 2008.

Gordon, Devin. "Anger Management: One Person Gave Ang Lee Trouble on 'The Hulk.'" *Newsweek*, June 16, 2003.

Hornaday, Ann. "A Director's Trip From Salad Days to a 'Banquet.'" *The New York Times*, August 1, 1993.

Kristof, Nicholas D. "Taiwan Becomes a Tiger with an Identity Crisis." *The New York Times*, January 12, 1992.

Lahr, John. "Becoming the Hulk." *The New Yorker*, June 30, 2003.

Lee, Min. "'Brokeback Mountain' Director's Roots Are in Rice-Growing Region." *AP Worldstream*, March 5, 2006.

Lim, Dennis. "Love as an Illusion: Beautiful to See, Impossible to Hold." *The New York Times*, August 26, 2007.

Lombardi, Kate Stone. "Far From the Spotlight, Winning Director's Wife." *The New York Times*, January 28, 2001.

Lyman, Rick. "Watching Movies with Ang Lee; Crouching Memory, Hidden Heart." *The New York Times*, March 9, 2001.

Mitchell, Elvis. "Ang Lee on Comic Books and Hulk as Hidden Dragon." *The New York Times*, June 22, 2003.

Moverman, Oren. "The Angle on Ang Lee." *Interview*, September 1, 1997.

Mowe, Richard. "The Year of the Dragon." *The Scotsman*, December 28, 2000.

Napach, Bernice. "Crouching Tiger, Hidden Editor." *The New York Times*, March 17, 2002.

Nichols, Peter M. "Home Video." *The New York Times*, January 5, 1996.

Nieves, Evelyn. "Heart of Suburban Darkness? Here. Uh-uh." *The New York Times*, November 30, 1997.

Proulx, Annie. "Blood on the Red Carpet." *The Guardian*, March 11, 2006.

Rea, Steven. "Ang Lee Returned to His Native Taiwan to Make 'Eat Drink Man Woman.'" *Knight Ridder/Tribune News Service*, August 19, 1994.

Schwartz, David. "A Pinewood Dialogue With Ang Lee and James Schamus." Museum of the Moving Image, June 7, 2003. Available online through *http://www.movingimage.us/pinewood*.

Simon, Scott. "Ang Lee Tackles Tough Subjects in 'Lust, Caution.'" *NPR Weekend Edition*, October 6, 2007.

Smith, Sean. "Forbidden Territory: In Ang Lee's Devastating Film 'Brokeback Mountain,' Jake Gyllenhaal and Heath Ledger Buck Hollywood Convention." *Newsweek*, November 21, 2005.

Spencer, Liese. "'Martial Arts Movies Are in My Blood.' Ang Lee Is Renowned for His Sensitivity, but Now Claims to Have Gone All Macho." *The Independent-London*, November 5, 1999.

Travers, Peter. "Crouching Tiger, Hidden Dragon." *Rolling Stone*, December 10, 2000.

Warren, Michael. "Ang Lee on a Roll: The Director of 'The Wedding Banquet' and 'Eat Drink Man Woman' Attempts an English Classic." *AsianWeek*, September 22, 1995.

Winters, Laura. "A Filmmaker Who Skates Across Cultures." *The Washington Post*, June 1, 1997.

FURTHER RESOURCES

BOOKS

Berry, Chris, and Mary Farquhar. *China on Screen: Cinema and Nation.* New York: Columbia University Press, 2006.

Cheshire, Ellen. *Ang Lee.* London: Pocket Essentials, 2001.

Lee, Ang. *Eat Drink Man Woman – The Wedding Banquet: Two Films by Ang Lee.* Woodstock, New York: Overlook Press, 1994.

Lowenstein, Stephen. *My First Movie: Twenty Celebrated Directors Talk About Their First Film.* New York: Pantheon, 2001.

Moody, Rick. *The Ice Storm.* New York: Little, Brown, 1994.

Proulx, Annie, Larry McMurtry, and Diana Ossana. *Brokeback Mountain: Story to Screenplay.* London: Harper Perennial, 2006.

WEB SITES

Ang Lee @ Filmbug
http://www.filmbug.com/db/781

Government Information Office, Republic of China (basic information on Taiwan)
http://www.gio.gov.tw

Sense of Cinema: Ang Lee
http://archive.sensesofcinema.com/contents/directors/08/ang-lee.html

PHOTO CREDITS

INDEX

ABOUT
THE AUTHOR

CLIFFORD W. MILLS is a writer, professor, and editor who specializes in biographies of world leaders, artists, literary figures, and sports legends. He is a film buff who lives in Jacksonville, Florida, and teaches literature at Columbia College.